Cambridge English

OFFICIAL

PRELIMINARY

PRELIMINARY ENGLISH TEST

8

WITH ANSWERS

AUTHENTIC EXAMINATION PAPERS
FROM CAMBRIDGE ENGLISH
LANGUAGE ASSESSMENT

520 117 83 4

Cambridge University Press
www.cambridge.org/elt

Cambridge English Language Assessment
www.cambridgeenglish.org

Information on this title: www.cambridge.org/9781107632233

© Cambridge University Press and UCLES 2014

It is normally necessary for written permission for copying to be obtained
in advance from a publisher. The sample answer sheets at the back of this
book are designed to be copied and distributed in class.
The normal requirements are waived here and it is not necessary to write to
Cambridge University Press for permission for an individual teacher to make copies
for use within his or her own classroom. Only those pages that carry the wording
'© UCLES 2014 Photocopiable' may be copied.

First published 2014
Reprinted 2014

Printed in the United Kingdom by Latimer Trend

A catalogue record for this publication is available from the British Library

ISBN 978-1-107-63223-3 Student's Book with answers
ISBN 978-1-107-67403-5 Student's Book without answers
ISBN 978-1-107-67243-7 Audio CDs (2)
ISBN 978-1-107-67583-4 Student's Book Pack (Student's Book with answers and Audio CDs (2))

The publishers have no responsibility for the persistence or accuracy
of URLs for external or third-party internet websites referred to in this publication,
and do not guarantee that any content on such websites is, or will remain,
accurate or appropriate. Information regarding prices, travel timetables, and other
factual information given in this work is correct at the time of first printing but
the publishers do not guarantee the accuracy of such information thereafter.

Contents

A Guide to Cambridge English: Preliminary

Cambridge English: Preliminary, also known as the *Preliminary English Test (PET)*, is part of a comprehensive range of exams developed by Cambridge English Language Assessment. Cambridge English exams have similar characteristics, but are designed for different purposes and different levels of English language ability. *Cambridge English: Preliminary* is at Level B1 (*Threshold*) of the Council of Europe's Common European Framework of Reference for Languages (CEFR). It has also been accredited in the UK as an Entry Level 3 Cambridge English Language Assessment certificate in the UK's National Qualifications Framework.

Examination	Council of Europe Framework Level	UK National Qualifications Framework Level
Cambridge English: Proficiency *Certificate of Proficiency in English (CPE)*	C2	3
Cambridge English: Advanced *Certificate in Advanced English (CAE)*	C1	2
Cambridge English: First *First Certificate in English (FCE)*	B2	1
Cambridge English: Preliminary *Preliminary English Test (PET)*	B1	Entry 3
Cambridge English: Key *Key English Test (KET)*	A2	Entry 2

Cambridge English: Preliminary is accepted by employers, and further education and government departments for business, study and immigration purposes. It is also useful preparation for higher level exams, such as *Cambridge English: First*, *Cambridge English: Advanced* and *Cambridge English: Proficiency*.

Cambridge English: Preliminary is ideal for learners who need to use English in a practical everyday way to communicate, e.g. read simple textbooks and articles, write simple personal letters, and deal with most of the situations you might meet when travelling in an English-speaking country.

Cambridge English: Preliminary is also available in a version with exam content and topics specifically targeted at the interests and experience of school-aged learners. *Cambridge English: Preliminary for Schools,* also known as *Preliminary English Test (PET) for Schools*, follows exactly the same format and level, and leads to the same certificate as *Cambridge English: Preliminary.*

Topics

These are the topics used in the *Cambridge English: Preliminary* exam:

Clothes	Hobbies and leisure	Relations with other people
Daily life	House and home	Services
Education	Language	Shopping
Entertainment and media	Natural world	Social interaction
Environment	People	Sport
Food and drink	Personal feelings, opinions	Transport
Free time	and experiences	Travel and holidays
Health, medicine and	Personal identification	Weather
exercise	Places and buildings	Work and jobs

Cambridge English: Preliminary content – an overview

Paper	Name	Timing	Content	Test focus
Paper 1	Reading/ Writing	1 hour 30 minutes	Reading: Five parts which test a range of reading skills with a variety of texts, ranging from very short notices to longer continuous texts. Writing: Three parts which test a range of writing skills.	Assessment of candidates' ability to understand the meaning of written English at word, phrase, sentence, paragraph and whole text level. Assessment of candidates' ability to produce straightforward written English, ranging from producing variations on simple sentences to pieces of continuous text.
Paper 2	Listening	35 minutes (plus 6 minutes transfer time)	Four parts ranging from short exchanges to longer dialogues and monologues.	Assessment of candidates' ability to understand dialogues and monologues in both informal and neutral settings on a range of everyday topics.
Paper 3	Speaking	10–12 minutes per pair of candidates	Four parts: In Part 1, candidates interact with an examiner; In Parts 2 and 4, they interact with another candidate; In Part 3, they have an extended individual long turn.	Assessment of candidates' ability to express themselves in order to carry out functions at *Threshold* level. To ask and to understand questions and make appropriate responses. To talk freely on matters of personal interest.

Paper 1: Reading and Writing

Paper format
The Reading component contains five parts. The Writing component contains three parts.

Number of questions
Reading has 35 questions; Writing has seven questions.

Sources
Authentic and adapted-authentic real world notices; newspapers and magazines; simplified encyclopaedias; brochures and leaflets; websites.

Answering

Candidates indicate answers by shading lozenges (Reading), or writing answers (Writing) on an answer sheet.

Timing

1 hour 30 minutes.

Marks

Reading: Each of the 35 questions carries one mark. This is weighted so that this comprises 25% of the total marks for the whole examination.

Writing: Questions 1–5 carry one mark each. Question 6 is marked out of five; and Question 7/8 is marked out of 20. This gives a total of 30 which is weighted so that it represents 25% of the total marks for the whole examination.

Preparing for the Reading component

To prepare for the Reading component, you should read a variety of authentic texts: for example, newspapers and magazines, non-fiction books, and other sources of factual material, such as leaflets, brochures and websites. It is also a good idea to practise reading (and writing) short communicative messages, including notes, cards and emails. Remember, you won't always need to understand every word in order to be able to do a task in the exam.

Before the examination, think about the time you need to do each part. It is usually approximately 50 minutes on the Reading component and 40 minutes on the Writing component.

Reading			
Part	Task Type and Format	Task Focus	Number of Questions
1	Three-option multiple choice. Five short discrete texts: signs and messages, postcards, notes, emails, labels, etc., plus one example.	Reading real-world notices and other short texts for the main message.	5
2	Matching. Five items in the form of descriptions of people to match to eight short adapted-authentic texts.	Reading multiple texts for specific information and detailed comprehension.	5
3	True/False. Ten items with an adapted-authentic long text.	Processing a factual text. Scanning for specific information while disregarding redundant material.	10
4	Four-option multiple choice. Five items with an adapted-authentic long text.	Reading for detailed comprehension: understanding attitude, opinion and writer purpose. Reading for gist, inference and global meaning.	5
5	Four-option multiple-choice cloze. Ten items, plus an integrated example, with an adapted-authentic text drawn from a variety of sources. The text is of a factual or narrative nature.	Understanding of vocabulary and grammar in a short text, and understanding the lexico-structural patterns in the text.	10

Preparing for the Writing component

Part 1

You have to complete five sentences which will test your grammar. There is an example, showing exactly what the task involves. You should write between one and three words to fill this gap. The second sentence, when complete, must mean the same as the first sentence.

It is essential to spell correctly and no marks will be given if a word is misspelled. You will also lose the mark if you produce an answer of more than three words, even if your writing includes the correct answer.

Part 2

You have to produce a short communicative message of between 35 and 45 words in length. You are told who you are writing to and why, and you must include three content points. These are clearly laid out with bullet points in the question. To gain top marks, all three points must be in your answer, so it is important to read the question carefully and plan what you will include. Marks will not be deducted for minor errors.

Before the exam, you need to practise writing answers of the correct length. Answers that are too short or too long and likely to contain irrelevant information will probably lose marks.

General Mark Scheme for Writing Part 2

Mark	Criteria
5	**All three parts of the message clearly communicated.**
	Only minor spelling errors or occasional grammatical errors.
4	**All three parts of the message communicated.**
	Some non-impeding errors in spelling and grammar, or some awkwardness of expression.
3	**All three parts of the message attempted.**
	Expression requires interpretation by the reader and contains impeding errors in spelling and grammar.
	All three parts of the message are included but the context is incorrect.
	OR
	Two parts of message are clearly communicated but one part is unattempted.
	Only minor spelling errors or occasional grammatical errors.
2	**Only two parts of the message communicated.**
	Some errors in spelling and grammar.
	The errors in expression may require patience and interpretation by the reader and impede communication.
	Some relevant content to **two or more points** but response is unclear.
1	**Only one part of the message communicated.**
	Some attempt to address the task but response is very unclear.
0	**Question unattempted or totally incomprehensible response.**

Part 3

You have a choice of task: either a story or an informal letter. You need to write about 100 words.

Make sure you practise enough before the exam. Reading simplified readers in English will give you ideas for story writing. Also writing to a penfriend or e-pal will give you useful practice.

Mark Scheme for Writing Part 3

Examiners look at four aspects of your writing: Content, Communicative Achievement, Organisation, and Language.

Content focuses on how well you have fulfilled the task, in other words if you have done what you were asked to do.

Communicative Achievement focuses on how appropriate the writing is for the letter or story and whether you have used the appropriate register.

Organisation focuses on the way you put the piece of writing together, in other words if it is logical and ordered, and the punctuation is correct.

Language focuses on your vocabulary and grammar. This includes the range of language, as well as how accurate it is.

For each of the subscales, the examiner gives a maximum of five marks; this gives an overall maximum score of 20 for the Part 3 task.

Examiners use the following assessment scale:

B1	Content	Communicative Achievement	Organisation	Language
5	All content is relevant to the task. Target reader is fully informed.	Uses the conventions of the communicative task to hold the target reader's attention and communicate straightforward ideas.	Text is generally well organised and coherent, using a variety of linking words and cohesive devices.	Uses a range of everyday vocabulary appropriately, with occasional inappropriate use of less common lexis. Uses a range of simple and some complex grammatical forms with a good degree of control. Errors do not impede communication.
4	*Performance shares features of Bands 3 and 5.*			
3	Minor irrelevances and/or omissions may be present. Target reader is on the whole informed.	Uses the conventions of the communicative task in generally appropriate ways to communicate straightforward ideas.	Text is connected and coherent, using basic linking words and a limited number of cohesive devices.	Uses everyday vocabulary generally appropriately, while occasionally overusing certain lexis. Uses simple grammatical forms with a good degree of control. While errors are noticeable, meaning can still be determined.
2	*Performance shares features of Bands 1 and 3.*			
1	Irrelevances and misinterpretation of task may be present. Target reader is minimally informed.	Produces text that communicates simple ideas in simple ways.	Text is connected using basic, high-frequency linking words.	Uses basic vocabulary reasonably appropriately. Uses simple grammatical forms with some degree of control. Errors may impede meaning at times.

B1	Content	Communicative Achievement	Organisation	Language
0	Content is totally irrelevant. Target reader is not informed.	*Performance below Band 1.*		

Length of responses
Make sure you write the correct amount of words. Responses which are too short may not have an adequate range of language and may not provide all the information that is required. Responses which are too long may contain irrelevant content and have a negative effect on the reader.

Varieties of English
You are expected to use a particular variety of English with some degree of consistency in areas such as spelling, and not for example switch from using a British spelling of a word to an American spelling of the same word.

Writing			
Part	**Task Type and Format**	**Task Focus**	**Number of Questions**
1	Sentence transformations. Five items, plus an integrated example, that are theme-related. Candidates are given sentences and then asked to complete similar sentences using a different structural pattern so that the sentence still has the same meaning.	Control and understanding of *Threshold/Cambridge English: Preliminary* grammatical structures. Rephrasing and reformulating information.	5
2	Short communicative message. Candidates are prompted to write a short message in the form of a postcard, note, email, etc. The prompt takes the form of a rubric to respond to.	A short piece of writing of 35–45 words focusing on communication of specific messages.	1
3	A longer piece of continuous writing. There is a choice of two questions, an informal letter or a story. Candidates are assessed on four aspects of their writing: Content, Communication Achievement, Organisation, and Language.	Writing about 100 words focusing on control and range of language.	1

Paper 2: Listening

Paper format
This paper contains four parts.

Number of questions
25

Text types
All texts are based on authentic situations.

Answering

Candidates indicate answers either by shading lozenges (Parts 1, 2 and 4) or writing answers (Part 3) on an answer sheet. Candidates record their answers on the question paper as they listen. They are then given six minutes at the end of the test to copy these on to the answer sheet.

Recording information

Each text is heard twice. Recordings will contain a variety of accents corresponding to standard variants of native speaker accents.

Timing

About 35 minutes, including six minutes to transfer answers.

Marks

Each question carries one mark. This gives a total of 25 marks, which represents 25% of the total marks for the whole examination.

Part	Task Type and Format	Task Focus	Number of questions
1	Multiple choice (discrete). Short neutral or informal monologues or dialogues. Seven discrete three-option multiple-choice items with visuals, plus one example.	Listening to identify key information from short exchanges.	7
2	Multiple choice. Longer monologue or interview (with one main speaker). Six three-option multiple-choice items.	Listening to identify specific information and detailed meaning.	6
3	Gap-fill. Longer monologue. Six gaps to fill in. Candidates need to write one or more words in each space.	Listening to identify, understand and interpret information.	6
4	True/False. Longer informal dialogue. Candidates need to decide whether six statements are correct or incorrect.	Listening for detailed meaning, and to identify the attitudes and opinions of the speakers.	6

Preparing for the Listening paper

You will hear the instructions for each task on the recording, and see them on the exam paper. In Part 1, there is also an example text and task to show you how to record your answers. In Parts 2, 3 and 4, the instructions are followed by a pause; you should read the questions in that part then. This will help you prepare for the listening.

The best preparation for the Listening paper is to listen to authentic spoken English at this level. Having discussions provides a good authentic source of listening practice, as does listening to the teacher. You can also listen to texts to give you practice in understanding different voices and styles of delivery.

Paper 3: Speaking

Paper format
The standard format is two candidates and two examiners. One of the examiners acts as an interlocutor and the other as an assessor. The interlocutor directs the test, while the assessor takes no part in the interaction.

Timing
10–12 minutes per pair of candidates.

Marks
Candidates are assessed on their performance throughout the test. There are a total of 25 marks in Paper 3, making 25% of the total score for the whole examination.

Part	Task Type and Format	Task Focus	Timing
1	Each candidate interacts with the interlocutor. The interlocutor asks the candidates questions in turn, using standardised questions.	Giving information of a factual, personal kind. The candidates respond to questions about present circumstances, past experiences and future plans.	2–3 minutes
2	Simulated situation. Candidates interact with each other. Visual stimulus is given to the candidates to aid the discussion task. The interlocutor sets up the activity using a standardised rubric.	Using functional language to make and respond to suggestions, discuss alternatives, make recommendations and negotiate agreement.	2–3 minutes
3	Extended turn. A colour photograph is given to each candidate in turn and they are asked to talk about it for up to a minute. Both photographs relate to the same topic.	Describing photographs and managing discourse, using appropriate vocabulary, in a longer turn.	3 minutes
4	General conversation. Candidates interact with each other. The topic of the conversation develops the theme established in Part 3. The interlocutor sets up the activity using a standardised rubric.	The candidates talk together about their opinions, likes/dislikes, preferences, experiences, habits, etc.	3 minutes

Assessment

Throughout the Speaking test, examiners listen to what you say and give you marks for how well you speak English, so you must try to speak about the tasks and answer the examiner and your partner's questions.

You are awarded marks by two examiners; the assessor and the interlocutor. The assessor awards marks from the Analytical Assessment scales for the following criteria:

Grammar and Vocabulary
This refers to how accurately you use grammar and also to the correct use of vocabulary. It also includes how wide a range of grammar and vocabulary you use.

Discourse Management

This refers to the length, relevance and coherence of your answers. You should be able to produce sentences which are clear and easy to follow. What you say should be related to the topic and the conversation in general.

Pronunciation

This refers to the how easy it is to understand what you say. You should be able to say words and sentences that are easy to understand.

Interactive Communication

This refers to how well you can talk about the task and to your partner and the examiner. You should be able to start the conversation and keep it going, and ask for repetition or clarification if needed.

B1	Grammar and Vocabulary	Discourse Management	Pronunciation	Interactive Communication
5	Shows a good degree of control of simple grammatical forms, and attempts some complex grammatical forms. Uses a range of appropriate vocabulary to give and exchange views on familiar topics.	Produces extended stretches of language despite some hesitation. Contributions are relevant despite some repetition. Uses a range of cohesive devices.	Is intelligible. Intonation is generally appropriate. Sentence and word stress is generally accurately placed. Individual sounds are generally articulated clearly.	Initiates and responds appropriately. Maintains and develops the interaction and negotiates towards an outcome with very little support.
4	*Performance shares features of Bands 3 and 5.*			
3	Shows a good degree of control of simple grammatical forms. Uses a range of appropriate vocabulary when talking about familiar topics.	Produces responses which are extended beyond short phrases, despite hesitation. Contributions are mostly relevant, but there may be some repetition. Uses basic cohesive devices.	Is mostly intelligible, and has some control of phonological features at both utterance and word levels.	Initiates and responds appropriately. Keeps the interaction going with very little prompting and support.
2	*Performance shares features of Bands 1 and 3.*			
1	Shows sufficient control of simple grammatical forms. Uses a limited range of appropriate vocabulary to talk about familiar topics.	Produces responses which are characterised by short phrases and frequent hesitation. Repeats information or digresses from the topic.	Is mostly intelligible, despite limited control of phonological features.	Maintains simple exchanges, despite some difficulty. Requires prompting and support.
0	*Performance below Band 1.*			

The examiner asking the questions (the interlocutor) gives marks for how well you do overall using a Global Achievement scale.

B1	Global Achievement
5	Handles communication on familiar topics, despite some hesitation. Organises extended discourse but occasionally produces utterances that lack coherence, and some inaccuracies and inappropriate usage occur.
4	*Performance shares features of Bands 3 and 5.*
3	Handles communication in everyday situations, despite hesitation. Constructs longer utterances but is not able to use complex language except in well-rehearsed utterances.
2	*Performance shares features of Bands 1 and 3.*
1	Conveys basic meaning in very familiar everyday situations. Produces utterances which tend to be very short – words or phrases – with frequent hesitation and pauses.
0	*Performance below Band 1.*

Further information

More information about *Cambridge English: Preliminary* or any other Cambridge English Language Assessment examination can be obtained from Cambridge English Language Assessment at the address below or from the website at www.cambridgeenglish.org.

Cambridge English Language Assessment
1 Hills Road
Cambridge CB1 2EU
United Kingdom

Telephone +44 1223 553997
Fax: +44 1223 553621
email: helpdesk@cambridgeenglish.org

Test 1

PAPER 1   READING AND WRITING   (1 hour 30 minutes)

READING

Part 1

Questions 1–5

Look at the text in each question.
What does it say?
Mark the correct letter **A**, **B** or **C** on your answer sheet.

Example:

0

A The six-week course is cheaper if you also do the one-day class.

B The one-day class is free for those who book the six-week course.

C You must pay for the six-week course before you do the one-day class.

Answer:

1

If Sally wants to go on the holiday she must

A send the details that were requested.

B contact the travel agency for further information.

C pay a deposit this evening.

2

Peter
The garage called. Your car is ready for collection. The key will be in their office until 5.30. Otherwise bring your spare key and get the other one another time.

✓ **A** Even if the garage is closed Peter can pick up his car.

✗ **B** Peter should reach the garage before 5.30 in order to collect his car.

C Peter cannot get his car until he collects the key.

3

Keep your bus ticket. Transport officers may request to see it at any time.

A If you lose your bus ticket, you should inform a transport officer.

✓ **B** There could be ticket checks during your bus journey.

C Passengers without a ticket may request one from a transport officer.

4

Paula
Can you give Lewis a ring at his home? I warned him you'd be back late but he said that didn't matter. I'm going out. See you tomorrow.
Jen

Jen says that

✓ **A** Lewis didn't know that Paula was away until tomorrow.

B Lewis doesn't mind what time Paula calls him at home.

C Lewis won't call Paula until late this evening.

5

Hunter Museum closed
Re-opens 15 September
Entry free
Guided tours only
Book early

From 15 September museum visitors

A will have to join a group.

✓ **B** will be free to go round alone.

C will have to pay for a tour guide.

Part 2

Questions 6–10

The people below all want to book a hotel in a European city.
On the opposite page there are descriptions of eight hotels in the city.
Decide which hotel would be the most suitable for the following people.
For questions **6–10**, mark the correct letter **(A–H)** on your answer sheet.

6

Nuala and Jaime want to celebrate their anniversary in a stylish hotel with good service. They plan to eat out, see a show and go sightseeing, without using public transport.

7

Sebastian wants to do some exercise at his hotel before attending a conference in the city centre. Afterwards he plans to walk back, have a meal in his room and relax for the evening.

8

Alex and Mel want a room in a traditional hotel with suitable facilities for their two children. They want to eat well before going sightseeing and want help with ideas for what to do.

9

Steve wants to stay overnight in a central hotel where he can experience the typical atmosphere of the city. He would like a light breakfast before leaving by public transport for his early morning flight.

10

Holly and Lucia are travelling round Europe and want to stay somewhere cheap and with nightlife nearby. They hope to make friends with other young travellers like themselves.

City Hotels

A   Royal

It's easy to miss this central hotel hidden away in a side street. Full of character, it is popular with families and business travellers but don't expect luxury service. Unlimited coffee, but nothing more, is available in the morning, but there are food stores a short walk away.

B   Mars

Hotel Mars is located on one of the main streets, a short walk from tourist attractions, theatres and restaurants. The luxury rooms are beautifully decorated and furnished with antiques. An excellent breakfast is served by waiters in the top-floor restaurant, which also offers spectacular evening views over the city.

C   Odeon

The Odeon proves that you can find an inexpensive hotel in one of the city's smartest locations but you'll need a taxi if you want to experience the city's nightlife. The rooms are comfortable but lack character. The buffet breakfast is average but with so many shops and cafés nearby it hardly matters.

D   Haussman

The wonderful city museum is right next door to this friendly 19th century hotel. The old-fashioned furniture and attractive iron balconies all add to the homely atmosphere. The hotel games room will keep all ages entertained, and there's plenty on offer at the self-service breakfast. Staff are always happy to supply information about what's on.

E   Windmill

This medium-priced hotel surrounded by artists' studios, lively bars and interesting food shops is right in the middle of the city. The underground station outside will take you anywhere, including the airport within minutes. Help yourself to breakfast from 8 am downstairs, or coffee and rolls can be brought to your room before that.

F   Stark's

A leading designer has decorated the inside of this smart modern hotel with bare grey walls, white bed covers and wooden floors. It's a half hour bus ride to the city centre or the airport. The ground floor has a top class restaurant and gym. Reception is open 24 hours a day.

G   Hi-Tech

All costs are kept low here. Guests book on the internet, then check in and buy everything they need from machines. Breakfast comes in airline-style boxes. You sleep in a tiny cabin for one and roll up your bed during the day. A fun choice for backpackers, who get together in the lively club next door.

H   Archway

This 19th century hotel is in a busy area with plenty of restaurants. It was modernised two years ago and now has a fitness centre. Rooms are very comfortable with widescreen TV. There's no restaurant, but you can order decent hot food via reception from the takeaway next door.

Part 3

Questions 11–20

Look at the sentences below about an unusual race along a river.
Read the text on the opposite page to decide if each sentence is correct or incorrect.
If it is correct, mark **A** on your answer sheet.
If it is not correct, mark **B** on your answer sheet.

---

11 Visitors come to Glen Nevis to enjoy outdoor activities all year round. A

12 Parts of the course of the River Race are less rough than others. A

13 Competitors are able to begin the race as soon as they are ready. B

14 The depth of the water has an effect on how long the races last. B

15 Some people return to do the race again and again. A

16 Only certain types of lilo may be used in the race. A

17 Competitors must use the safety clothing provided by race organisers. B

18 The most frightening part of the race is in the second half of the course. A

19 Members of the mountain rescue team are paid professionals. A

20 There is a fixed charge for visitors who come to see the race. B

The Glen Nevis River Race

Glen Nevis is known as the 'outdoor capital' of Scotland. Britain's highest mountain, Ben Nevis, rises above the area, while the waters of the River Nevis flow through the rocky valley below. The spectacular scenery attracts walkers and climbers all through the seasons, despite the cold weather in winter.

During the summer months, one of the most exciting activities is the annual Glen Nevis River Race, in which competitors race for three kilometres along the river, but not in a boat. Instead, each competitor uses a lilo, a plastic bed filled with air normally used for camping or floating in the sea, or another kind of beach toy to race along the river. There are rocks, waterfalls and sections with scary names like Dead Dog Pool and the Leg Breaker for them to get through though there are areas of calmer waters too.

Competitors set off at 30 second intervals by jumping with their lilos from a tiny shelf in a rock into the fast-flowing water 12 metres below. It can take anything from 20 minutes to over two hours to complete the course, depending on the level of the river and the abilities of the competitor.

There is much discussion amongst people who take part regularly about which type of lilo works best for the race. Some prefer short wide ones, while others say that a long narrow one is better. But since you can use anything that floats, all kinds of beach toys such as bananas, sharks and crocodiles can be seen floating down the river.

The only rules are that competitors must be at least 16 years old, and should provide their own crash helmet, a rubber wet suit and a life jacket. Gloves and old trainers are recommended to protect against knocks and bumps. The most important qualification, however, is a sense of fun.

The race is full of exciting moments, and the greatest of these is at the Lower Falls Leap, where terrified competitors have to jump over a ten-metre waterfall not far from the finish. More than 3,000 athletes have taken part in the race during its 30-year history. Their £30 entry fee helps to raise money for the mountain rescue team, whose members provide an essential service in the region for free. The race is a popular afternoon out for visitors and it costs nothing to watch, although any money given is gratefully accepted.

The prizes may not be fantastic, but everyone receives a certificate of completion and the winner gets the title River Race Champion and all agree that it has been worth it for the satisfying feeling of reaching the end safely.

Part 4

Questions 21–25

Read the text and questions below.
For each question, mark the correct letter **A**, **B**, **C** or **D** on your answer sheet.

Cliff Jones

In 2005, Cliff Jones began a journey round Britain on a unicycle, a bike with only one wheel. He had already made a documentary film about his experiences travelling round Europe in a 50-year-old car. He was mad about motor sport and had a job building racing car engines. To save money, Cliff rode to work in London on an old bicycle, which he also used to go to France on holiday. 'That trip opened my eyes,' he says. 'I decided to do a tour of Britain by bike.'

Cliff didn't want a normal touring bike, and he knew he wanted to build one himself. 'The craziest bicycle I could think of was a unicycle, so I went to a factory to see how they are made.' After one false start in 2004, when he had to turn back because of a knee injury, he finally set out in 2005. He was away for four months, and travelled over 8,500 km.

The best bit of the trip was arriving in Wales and seeing Mount Snowdon. 'Although I met cyclists who could easily ride up mountains on their bikes, which I couldn't do, I never regretted my unicycle. The further away from London I got, the more amazed people seemed by it.' His worst moment came when he had to drink some dirty water from a stream. A serious fever kept him in bed in hospital for five long days. He was determined not to give up and go back home before he had completed his challenge, but found it hard to carry on because he felt so weak. Yet despite all this, Cliff now says, 'If I could afford it, I would like to do something similar again.'

---

21   What is the writer trying to do in this text?
    A   advise people to take adventure holidays
    B   explain a rather unusual choice of transport
    C   suggest the benefits of a special vehicle
    D   persuade people to travel long distances

22 What made Cliff realise he wanted to cycle round Britain?

    A   touring Europe in an old car

    B   visiting a unicycle factory

    C   attending motor races abroad

    D   taking his bike to another country ✓

23 When Cliff met other cyclists in the mountains, he was

    A   anxious to get away from them.

    B   satisfied with his own type of bicycle. ✓

    C   jealous of what they were able to do.

    D   surprised by their attitude towards him.

24 What was Cliff's biggest problem during the trip?

    A   He fell ill for nearly a week. ✓

    B   He had to go home to rest.

    C   He wanted to finish his trip early.

    D   He took too long to get to one place.

25 What might Cliff say after his trip?

    A

> My aim was to get to the top of Mount Snowdon, so I was disappointed not to reach Wales.

    B

> I'm already building the unicycle for my next trip. It's going to be the latest model so I can ride up mountains.

    C

> I was happy when I managed to get started at the second attempt. Fortunately, my knee didn't give me any more trouble.

    D

> I'm lucky that I have plenty of money. That means I can set off on another trip whenever I like. ✓

Part 5

Questions 26–35

Read the text below and choose the correct word for each space.
For each question, mark the correct letter **A**, **B**, **C** or **D** on your answer sheet.

Example:

0   **A** brought   **B** held   **C** kept   **D** grown

Answer:
0	A B C D

Alpacas

Alpacas were first **(0)** .... by the Inca people in the mountains of South America, more than six thousand years ago. These animals **(26)** .... clothes, food and fuel for their owners. The softest wool was **(27)** .... worn by the leaders of Incan society though.

When Spanish explorers **(28)** .... in the fifteenth century, sheep were introduced and these gradually **(29)** .... alpacas in the region. It wasn't **(30)** .... the middle of the 20th century that both farmers and fashion designers began to recognise the **(31)** .... of alpacas again. They are easy to look **(32)** .... since they eat grass and are used to low temperatures. Their wool, which comes in a **(33)** .... of natural colours from white to dark brown, is lighter and warmer than sheep's wool and **(34)** .... strong.

It is not surprising **(35)** .... that alpacas are becoming a familiar sight in the fields of North America, Australia and the UK.

26	**A** supported	**B** provided	**C** turned	**D** gained
27	**A** mainly	**B** fully	**C** extremely	**D** absolutely
28	**A** reached	**B** delivered	**C** arrived	**D** transferred
29	**A** retired	**B** removed	**C** returned	**D** replaced
30	**A** until	**B** after	**C** during	**D** before
31	**A** prizes	**B** rewards	**C** qualities	**D** points
32	**A** at	**B** after	**C** for	**D** like
33	**A** row	**B** group	**C** range	**D** crowd
34	**A** only	**B** also	**C** instead	**D** too
35	**A** therefore	**B** already	**C** otherwise	**D** enough

WRITING

Part 1

Questions 1–5

Here are some sentences about a baseball game.
For each question, complete the second sentence so that it means the same as the first.
Use no more than three words.
Write only the missing words on your answer sheet.
You may use this page for any rough work.

Example:

0   Baseball is more popular than any other sport in the USA.

Baseball is the .... **popular sport in the USA.**

Answer: | 0 | *most* |

---

1   Nick was given a ticket to a baseball game by his friend Akio.

Nick's friend Akio .... **him a ticket to a baseball game.**

2   Nick had never been to a baseball game before.

It was the .... **Nick had been to a baseball game.**

3   Nick wasn't sure when the match would finish.

Nick wasn't sure .... **long the match would go on for.**

4   In the game the Dolphins team played better than the Giants.

In the game the Giants team didn't play as .... **the Dolphins.**

5   Now Nick can't wait for the next game.

Now Nick is really looking .... **to the next game.**

Part 2

Question 6

You planned to meet your friend, Robin, in town to go shopping, but Robin didn't arrive.

Write an email to Robin. In your email, you should

- ask why Robin didn't arrive
- explain how you felt
- suggest another time to go shopping together.

Write **35–45 words** on your answer sheet.

Part 3

Write an answer to **one** of the questions (**7** or **8**) in this part.
Write your answer in about **100 words** on your answer sheet.
Tick the box (Question 7 or Question 8) on your answer sheet to show which question you have answered.

Question 7

- This is part of a letter you receive from an English friend.

> I've just finished reading a really good book. What kinds of thing do you enjoy reading? Do you prefer books or magazines? Tell me something about a famous writer from your country.

- Now write a letter answering your friend's questions.
- Write your **letter** in about 100 words on your answer sheet.

Question 8

- Your English teacher wants you to write a story.
- This is the title for your story:

An unexpected visitor

- Write your **story** in about 100 words on your answer sheet.

PAPER 2   LISTENING   approx 35 minutes
(including 6 minutes transfer time)

Part 1

Questions 1–7

There are seven questions in this part.
For each question there are three pictures and a short recording.
Choose the correct picture and put a tick (✓) in the box below it.

Example: Where did the man leave his camera?

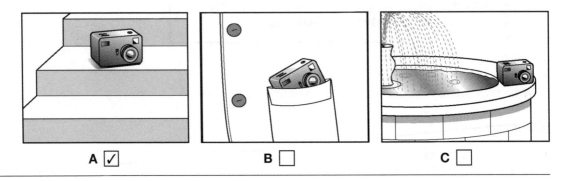

A ✓   B ☐   C ☐

1   What did the man buy?

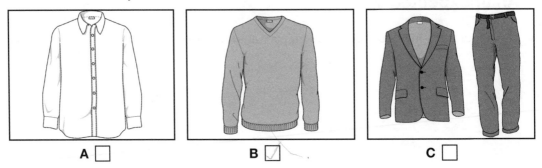

A ☐   B ☑   C ☐

2   How will the woman help the man?

A ☐   B ☐   C ☑

3 What will the students buy for their teacher?

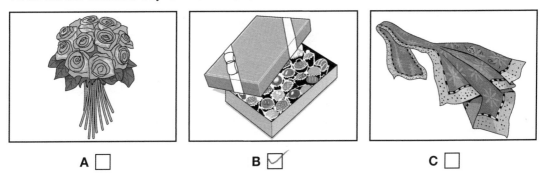

A ☐   B ☑   C ☐

4 Which exhibition is the busiest today?

A ☑   B ☐   C ☐

5 Where can visitors see the ducks?

A ☐   B ☐   C ☑

6 What will the weather be like when the festival starts?

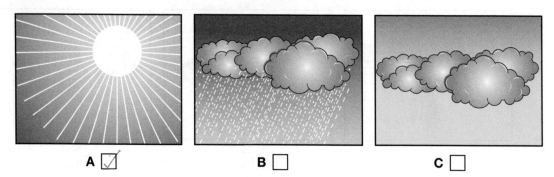

A ☑   B ☐   C ☐

7 What has the man sent back to the company?

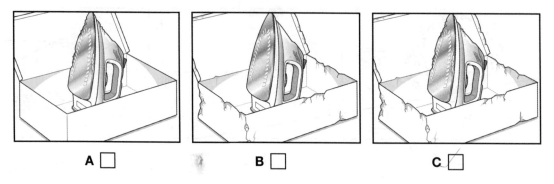

A ☐   B ☐   C ☐

Part 2

Questions 8–13

You will hear an interview with a man called Tim Jones, who organises an international summer course for young musicians.
For each question, put a tick (✓) in the correct box.

---

8   What does Tim enjoy most about his job?   **A**   sorting out all the details   ☑

  B   getting to know the musicians   ☐

  C   listening to lots of good music   ☐

9   Young musicians who want to do the course   **A**   need to fill in an online form.   ☑

  B   have to perform to a very high level.   ☐

  C   must be able to speak English very well.   ☑

10   Tim says that the teachers on the course   **A**   usually enjoy themselves.   ☑

  B   are always complaining.   ☐

  C   are extremely well-paid.   ☐

11   Tim likes to hold the course in a place which   **A**   is specially designed for musicians.   ☐

  B   is convenient for public transport.   ☑

  C   is a long way from a big city.   ☐

12 What does Tim say about musical instruments?

    A Students cannot bring expensive ones. ☐

    B Students sometimes lose them. ☑

    C Students keep them in a special place. ☐

13 What does Tim say about the concert tour after the course?

    A It has to make a lot of money. ☐

    B It needs to be carefully planned. ☑

    C It's difficult to sell tickets. ☐

Part 3

Questions 14–19

You will hear an announcement about a train trip through a desert.
For each question, fill in the missing information in the numbered space.

Desert Train Trip

The time the trip takes is **(14)** ....

In the past, Oldsville had an important **(15)** .... industry.

Passengers can see pretty **(16)** .... close to the train.

There are some attractive **(17)** .... to see under an old bridge.

In a small store on the train, **(18)** .... are on sale.

Today, refreshments will be for sale in a **(19)** .... instead of from a machine.

Part 4

Questions 20–25

Look at the six sentences for this part.
You will hear a woman called Julie and a man called Greg talking about an indoor wildlife centre they have visited.
Decide if each sentence is correct or incorrect.
If it is correct, put a tick (✓) in the box under **A** for **YES**. If it is not correct, put a tick (✓) in the box under **B** for **NO**.

		A YES	B NO
20	They agree that the wildlife centre building is well designed.	☐	☐
21	Julie thought the sharks at the wildlife centre were frightening.	☐	☑
22	Julie found the building was too warm.	☐	☐
23	Greg was disappointed with the number of insects.	☐	☑
24	Greg only managed to see one tree frog.	☐	☐
25	Julie is very keen to return to the wildlife centre.	☑	☐

About the Speaking test

The Speaking test lasts about 10 to 12 minutes. You take the test with another candidate. There are two examiners in the room. One examiner talks to you and the other examiner listens to you. Both the examiners give you marks.

Part 1

The examiners introduce themselves and then one examiner asks you and your partner to say your names and spell them. This examiner then asks you questions about yourself, your daily life, interests, etc.

Part 2

The examiner asks you to talk about something together and gives you a drawing to help you.

Part 3

You each have a chance to talk by yourselves. The examiner gives you a colour photograph to look at and asks you to talk about it. When you have finished talking, the examiner gives your partner a different photograph to look at and to talk about.

Part 4

The examiner asks you and your partner to say more about the subject of the photographs in Part 3. You may be asked to give your opinion or to talk about something that has happened to you.

Test 2

PAPER 1   READING AND WRITING (1 hour 30 minutes)

READING

Part 1

Questions 1–5

Look at the text in each question.
What does it say?
Mark the correct letter **A**, **B** or **C** on your answer sheet.

Example:

0

A The six-week course is cheaper if you also do the one-day class.

B The one-day class is free for those who book the six-week course.

C You must pay for the six-week course before you do the one-day class.

Answer:

1

A Liz plans to go shopping with Kate tonight.

B Liz needs Ted to buy some ingredients for her.

C Liz wants some advice on how to make vegetable soup.

2

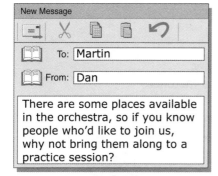

New Message

To: Martin
From: Dan

There are some places available in the orchestra, so if you know people who'd like to join us, why not bring them along to a practice session?

Dan is trying

A to persuade Martin to join the orchestra.

B to increase the number of people in the orchestra.

C to get help from people to set up an orchestra.

3

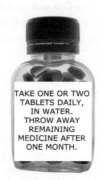

TAKE ONE OR TWO TABLETS DAILY, IN WATER. THROW AWAY REMAINING MEDICINE AFTER ONE MONTH.

A You should take this medicine twice daily for a month.

B You should finish all of this medicine within one month.

C You should get rid of any medicine that is left after a month.

4

> **FREE!**
> PIZZA FROM OUR CAFÉ WITH EVERY CINEMA TICKET BOUGHT FROM OUR TICKET DESK!

Cinema-goers can

A collect a free pizza at the cinema ticket desk.

B go into the cinema for free if they buy pizza from the café.

C get pizza for nothing when they pay to go into the cinema.

5

> Sarah,
> I've left my handbag at the office, so I'm just walking back to get it. Wait for me at the café – I won't be long!
> Anna

A Anna is going to be late getting to the café.

B Anna has forgotten the way to the café.

C Anna is collecting Sarah's handbag from the café.

Part 2

Questions 6–10

The people below all want to go on a visit to a guitar factory.
On the opposite page there are descriptions of eight guitar factories.
Decide which factory would be the most suitable for the following people.
For questions **6–10**, mark the correct letter **(A–H)** on your answer sheet.

6

Ken wants to visit a factory where he can discuss guitar-making with people who make them. He'd like to hear music played live, and visit somewhere nearby that's connected to rock music.

7

Maria wants to visit a factory that sells low-priced guitars. She'd also like to see some old ones that were played by well-known guitar heroes, and learn how they were created for individual musicians.

8

Juan wants to learn to make guitars, and would like information on a career doing this. He'd like to see the different production stages, and try playing some instruments.

9

Tomas and Helena want advice on getting a guitar made for their musician son. They want to stay and eat while they're at the guitar factory, and to buy souvenirs for their grandchildren.

10

Sara is studying the history of music, and wants to learn more about how guitars were first designed, and how materials are chosen for them. She'd also like to buy a book about guitar-making.

Guitar factory

A Rockalls

The café at Rockalls is always a lively place to be – great music played live on instruments made at this well-known guitar factory. Its location is surprising though, as it's miles from the nearest town – but it's definitely well worth the trip.

B Ronsons

Ronsons have their own museum full of the guitars they've made for rock stars. Your guide will tell you about the skills used to make sure that each guitar was exactly what its owner wanted. After the tour, go and visit the Ronsons shop where guitars are available at better discounts than you'll find in other shops.

C Barnards

Barnards are well known for the individual design of their guitars, ideal for professional players with money to spend. You can discuss your needs with staff, who'll make the perfect instrument for you. After your factory tour, relax in the café, before visiting the shop which has gifts for every age.

D Stocktons

The staff at Stocktons are always happy to talk to interested visitors about the love and care that goes into designing and making their stylish modern guitars. The shop has a fantastic selection of books on the guitar to choose from, as well as guitars of course.

E PSA

Staff at PSA have made guitars by hand since 1956, and they'll answer any questions about their work. Visit the factory shop after your tour or watch professional players performing on PSA guitars in the café. There's also the chance to go and see the homes of several rock stars that lived in this area.

F Maxwells

Maxwells have made guitars for over 100 years. In their museum, you can find out about the early development of the guitar, and see how much care still goes into selecting the wood that's used to create perfect guitars. And don't forget the gift shop, with its huge selection of books on the guitar.

G Delamere

The shop at the Delamere factory is worth a visit as guitars are for sale at lower than average prices, plus there's plenty of advice about what to buy. There is little else on offer though after your visit and apart from the shop the factory offers few visitor facilities.

H Mitchells

Mitchells train their staff to become as skilled as possible in the art of guitar-making – and encourage people who are considering this as a profession. You'll get the opportunity to watch exactly how each guitar is put together, and you can even have a go at playing one or two!

Part 3

Questions 11–20

Look at the sentences below about a centre where visitors can go to watch the stars.
Read the text on the opposite page to decide if each sentence is correct or incorrect.
If it is correct, mark **A** on your answer sheet.
If it is not correct, mark **B** on your answer sheet.

___

11   The Tracker Star-Watching Centre is right at the top of a mountain.

12   There is a variety of ticket prices that you can choose from.

13   You can attend various courses at the Centre during the day.

14   You are allowed to use the Centre's special equipment by yourself to see the stars.

15   Centre employees will help you to notice the best sights in the sky.

16   Visitors will get different views of the planet Saturn, depending on when they visit.

17   A telescope is needed to see all the objects that the staff show you.

18   Some students from a nearby university can answer the questions you have.

19   You can buy something to wear at the Centre if you feel too cold.

20   Visitors who need fuel for their vehicles can get some on the way up the mountain.

Tracker Star-Watching Centre

Are you interested in finding out more about the stars and planets in the night skies? Then come and join us at the Tracker Star-Watching Centre halfway up Mintal Mountain. We hold popular star-watching sessions almost every night of the year from 6.00 until 10.00. The Centre is run entirely on money given to us by the public, so although there's no actual charge for your tickets, we're always grateful when people choose to give us large or small amounts of money – it all helps. And if after one of our evening sessions you become interested in finding out more, and you're willing to pay a small fee, then we run a range of daytime courses.

During our evening programmes, you'll first see a documentary that tells you all about the history of the Centre and all the star watching programmes that we run here, and then you'll move outside where several special telescopes are set up for you to see the stars in more detail. Our expert staff will manage all the equipment and during the evening they will guide you so that you get to see the most interesting objects, including double stars and planets. You may also get a chance to see the planet Saturn, with its glowing rings though its brightness changes throughout the year. We're so far up that the clouds are often below us, so our view of the night skies is clear and bright. We'll also tell you about some of the most important things that can be seen in the night sky without equipment. There are always students from the university here who help out at the Tracker Centre in their spare time, and are prepared to give you any information you want about the stars.

Visitors to the Centre should note that we often experience near-freezing night-time temperatures at the Centre, so please dress in warm clothes. However, if you have a problem and find you are not warm enough, sweaters and scarves, which might make a nice souvenir, are available from the Centre store.

Visitors should also make sure they have a full tank of petrol in their vehicles before making the trip up to the Centre, as petrol is unavailable near the station, and the nearest petrol stations are about 40 km away. The 12 km climb to the Centre can take some time – so make sure your car is in good enough condition to make it! We hope to see you at the Tracker Centre soon!

Part 4

Questions 21–25

Read the text and questions below.
For each question, mark the correct letter **A**, **B**, **C** or **D** on your answer sheet.

James Waltham – Chocolate Taster

Whenever I tell people what I do for a living, they can hardly believe this job exists. But I'm not joking! I spend my days at work eating chocolate! Tasting the chocolate is an essential part of making sure that customers get perfect bars of high-quality chocolate from the company I work for.

Every week I receive samples, small amounts that show what the chocolate is like, from our factory and I have to check them for taste, texture and smell. I also have to taste the raw materials we usually use – the nuts, fruit and so on. I spend days choosing the most suitable ones to go into the chocolate.

Just beside my company office I have a kitchen where I can test and taste products I make – and I keep my colleagues happy by giving them samples! My kitchen is full of machines and ingredients to play with. It's wonderful to have a private space I can go off to during the day.

No two days are the same in this job. Sometimes I am at our food lab and others I'm out of the country buying our raw materials and as I've got a young family that can be difficult. But that kind of variety, and lack of routine, is something I love about the job, although I think it still comes second to the chocolate itself! The question I get asked most is whether I get bored of chocolate. I've worked with it for a long time, and I've never felt I didn't want to eat it. In fact, I'll often go home and eat some more in the evening!

21   What is James Waltham doing in the text?

    A   recommending the best ways to test chocolate
    B   describing what personal qualities are needed to do his job
    C   telling readers what makes his job worth doing for him
    D   suggesting different methods of making chocolate

22   James says that when he tells people about his work, they

    A   say they would like to do the same thing.
    B   doubt whether he is serious.
    C   think it must be very easy.
    D   wonder why he chose it as a career.

23 James says that working in his kitchen involves

    A   trying various different preparation methods.

    B   checking the quantities of ingredients in each bar.

    C   discussing his opinions with other members of staff.

    D   making sure the best chocolate-making equipment is used.

24 What does James think is a disadvantage of his job?

    A   He sometimes feels he has eaten too much chocolate.

    B   He finds it difficult to have a routine with his work.

    C   He has worked with the same product too long.

    D   He needs to travel abroad some of the time.

25 Which one would be an advert for the chocolate company James works for?

A

> Every single bar of chocolate that leaves our factory is tested for its taste.

B

> We choose only the best ingredients – just chocolate beans, sugar and milk. We don't add anything else.

C

> We're proud of being so environmentally friendly - all our ingredients are bought from local businesses.

D

> We check everything that goes into our chocolate, so that you can enjoy the best chocolate possible.

Part 5

Questions 26–35

Read the text below and choose the correct word for each space.
For each question, mark the correct letter **A**, **B**, **C** or **D** on your answer sheet.

Example:

| 0 | **A** valuable | **B** typical | **C** original | **D** suitable |

Answer:

0	A B C D
	■ ☐ ☐ ☐

Horses

Horses have been **(0)** .... to humans for thousands of years. Because there are several different **(26)** .... of horses such as coldbloods, which are large but gentle, or hotbloods that are **(27)** .... for their running ability, there are horses for every purpose. We use them for transport as **(28)** .... as for physical work, for example **(29)** .... farm machinery. It's now also very **(30)** .... to see horses used in sports.

Horses need food and water in large **(31)** .... A horse can drink **(32)** .... twenty and forty litres of water a day, and around a kilo of food for **(33)** .... fifty kilos of its body weight. Horses need to be out in the fields, as grass is part of their diet.

They can live for **(34)** .... 25 years, so their owners need to give them **(35)** .... of love and attention – but horses always give lots back.

26	**A** makes	**B** styles	**C** marks	**D** sorts
27	**A** known	**B** noticed	**C** familiar	**D** realised
28	**A** long	**B** far	**C** well	**D** soon
29	**A** going	**B** pulling	**C** taking	**D** doing
30	**A** obvious	**B** clear	**C** common	**D** regular
31	**A** totals	**B** sums	**C** numbers	**D** amounts
32	**A** from	**B** between	**C** about	**D** beyond
33	**A** both	**B** any	**C** every	**D** all
34	**A** after	**B** through	**C** over	**D** towards
35	**A** plenty	**B** more	**C** full	**D** enough

WRITING

Part 1

Questions 1–5

Here are some sentences about a cycling trip to the countryside.
For each question, complete the second sentence so that it means the same as the first.
Use no more than three words.
Write only the missing words on your answer sheet.
You may use this page for any rough work.

Example:

0 Cycling is great fun and it's good for you.

Cycling is great fun as .... **as being good for you.**

Answer:

0	*well*

---

1 I often go cycling with my friend Dan at the weekends.

My friend Dan usually .... **cycling with me at the weekends.**

2 Our favourite place to visit is the lake near our town.

We like visiting the lake near our town .... **than anywhere else.**

3 We hadn't cycled into the countryside for several months.

It was several months .... **we had cycled into the countryside.**

4 We only had a break when we got hungry at about 2.00.

We didn't have a break .... **we got hungry at about 2.00.**

5 It was the best ride we'd had for a long time.

We hadn't had .... **a good ride for a long time.**

Part 2

Question 6

You are on holiday in a town by the sea. You decide to write a postcard to your friend, Sam.

Write a postcard to Sam. In your postcard, you should

- explain why you chose this town for a holiday
- describe something you have enjoyed doing on your holiday
- arrange to meet Sam when you return.

Write **35–45 words** on your answer sheet.

Part 3

Write an answer to **one** of the questions (**7** or **8**) in this part.
Write your answer in about **100 words** on your answer sheet.
Tick the box (**Question 7** or **Question 8**) on your answer sheet to show which question you have answered.

Question 7

- This is part of a letter you receive from an Australian friend.

> I've just joined a film club. We watch and discuss films from different countries. What kinds of films are popular in your country? Can you suggest a good film for our club to watch? Why do you like it?

- Now write a letter answering your friend's questions.
- Write your **letter** in about 100 words on your answer sheet.

Question 8

- Your English teacher wants you to write a story.
- This is the title for your story:

A bus journey I'll never forget

- Write your **story** in about 100 words on your answer sheet.

PAPER 2 LISTENING approx 35 minutes
(including 6 minutes transfer time)

Part 1

Questions 1–7

There are seven questions in this part.
For each question there are three pictures and a short recording.
Choose the correct picture and put a tick (✓) in the box below it.

Example: Where did the man leave his camera?

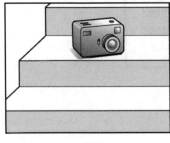 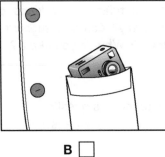 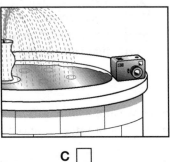

A ✓   B ☐   C ☐

---

1   Which part of the Arts Centre only opened recently?

A ☐   B ☐   C ☐

2   What does the shop assistant give the man?

A ☐

B ☐

C ☐

3   Where does the woman feel pain?

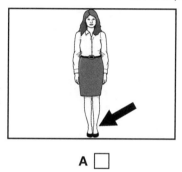
A ☐

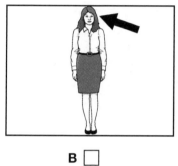
B ☐

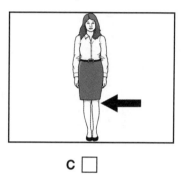
C ☐

4   Where must the woman go to buy dollars?

A ☐

B ☐

C ☐

5   Which vegetable is used in all today's recipes?

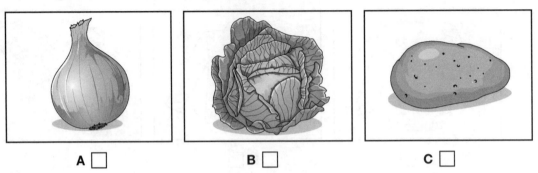

A ☐   **B** ☐   **C** ☐

6   Where is the meeting?

A ☐   **B** ☐   **C** ☐

7   How did the man want to pay?

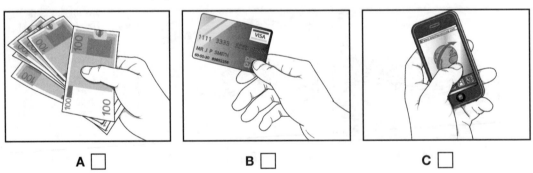

A ☐   **B** ☐   **C** ☐

Part 2

Questions 8–13

You will hear an interview with a woman called Marta Stanston, who runs a mobile restaurant that she sets up in different places.
For each question, put a tick (✓) in the correct box.

8   What did Marta dislike about her first job?
   A   It was really badly paid. ☐
   B   The boss didn't listen to her. ☐
   C   She found the staff unfriendly. ☐

9   At first, what did Marta find most surprising about mobile restaurants?
   A   They are only advertised online. ☐
   B   Food never gets thrown away. ☐
   C   Menus can be easily changed. ☐

10   For Marta, the best thing about mobile restaurants was
   A   knowing she would have customers. ☐
   B   being able to work outdoors. ☐
   C   finding that waiters weren't needed. ☐

11   Marta had difficulty serving food on a beach because of
   A   the sun. ☐
   B   the rain. ☐
   C   the wind. ☐

12 Marta tries to avoid serving meals in her home because

    A she doesn't have enough furniture. ☐

    B the neighbours have complained. ☐

    C there is a lack of space. ☐

13 What worries Marta about the future?

    A mobile restaurants going out of fashion ☐

    B the wrong people opening restaurants like hers ☐

    C health inspectors coming to her restaurant ☐

Part 3

Questions 14–19

You will hear an announcement about an outdoor cinema.
For each question, fill in the missing information in the numbered space.

Outdoor cinema

The cinema is surrounded by **(14)** .... and there are beautiful views.

It's possible to watch the **(15)** .... during a film.

Cinema visitors are advised to take a **(16)** .... with them to sit on.

The cinema is **(17)** .... kilometres from the city if you go on foot.

It's a good idea to have a **(18)** .... when the film is over.

Cinema tickets can be bought online at www.**(19)** .... org.

Part 4

Questions 20–25

Look at the six sentences for this part.
You will hear a woman called Laura and a man called Karl talking about living away from home whilst studying at university.
Decide if each sentence is correct or incorrect.
If it is correct, put a tick (✓) in the box under **A** for **YES**. If it is not correct, put a tick (✓) in the box under **B** for **NO**.

		A YES	B NO
20	Karl says it's been difficult finding somewhere to live.	☐	☐
21	Karl has had problems studying in another language.	☐	☐
22	Laura is surprised at how little work there is on her course.	☐	☐
23	Karl is uncertain whether to return home after his course.	☐	☐
24	Laura is missing her parents.	☐	☐
25	Laura feels that she's too busy to visit Karl.	☐	☐

About the Speaking test

The Speaking test lasts about 10 to 12 minutes. You take the test with another candidate. There are two examiners in the room. One examiner talks to you and the other examiner listens to you. Both the examiners give you marks.

Part 1

The examiners introduce themselves and then one examiner asks you and your partner to say your names and spell them. This examiner then asks you questions about yourself, your daily life, interests, etc.

Part 2

The examiner asks you to talk about something together and gives you a drawing to help you.

Part 3

You each have a chance to talk by yourselves. The examiner gives you a colour photograph to look at and asks you to talk about it. When you have finished talking, the examiner gives your partner a different photograph to look at and to talk about.

Part 4

The examiner asks you and your partner to say more about the subject of the photographs in Part 3. You may be asked to give your opinion or to talk about something that has happened to you.

Test 3

PAPER 1   READING AND WRITING   (1 hour 30 minutes)

READING

Part 1

Questions 1–5

Look at the text in each question.
What does it say?
Mark the correct letter **A**, **B** or **C** on your answer sheet.

Example:

0

New Message
To: Felipe
From: Anastasia
Won't be able to get to tonight's show. The roads are still icy and they're forecasting snow. Why not take your sister instead?

Anastasia is writing to say

A the weather will make her miss tonight's show.

B tonight's show is cancelled due to bad weather.

C Felipe should watch the weather forecast tonight.

Answer: 0

1

Karen,
Your French teacher rang earlier – the Tuesday evening class you wanted next term is full, but Thursday's available if you can go then instead. He'll ring back later.
Jan

A Karen has the possibility of attending French classes on two evenings per week.

B Karen's evening classes will now start at an earlier time this term.

C Karen needs to decide whether to change the evening that she has classes.

2

> LOCAL FARMERS
> SUPPLY ALL THIS
> SUPERMARKET'S
> VEGETABLES – KEEPING
> PRICES LOW
> FOR OUR CUSTOMERS!

A We get fresh vegetables from the farmers with the cheapest prices.

B We promise you won't find lower-priced fresh food than ours.

C We buy our fresh vegetables locally to save you money.

3

Jack,
My car broke down on the motorway, so I'll be late picking you up. I'm on the way again now - see you at your house in 30 minutes.
David

A David is fixing his broken car on the motorway at the moment.

B David is half an hour away from where Jack lives.

C David is hoping Jack will collect him in his car soon.

4

New Message

To: Denise
From: Maria

About that sweater you borrowed for skiing last time – could you bring it round to my place? I'm going snowboarding with Mark soon and it'll be cold!

A Maria needs Denise to return something she lent her a while ago.

B Maria is inviting Denise to go somewhere with her and Mark.

C Maria wants to borrow something from Denise that she can wear for snowboarding.

5

> **PARKING**
>
> HOSPITAL VISITORS ONLY
> WAITING LIMITED TO
> TWO HOURS
> FOLLOW SIGNS TO STAFF
> PARKING

A Only hospital visitors can park here for longer than two hours.

B Members of hospital staff are allowed to leave their cars here.

C This car park is for people visiting the hospital for a short time.

Part 2

Questions 6–10

The people below all want to visit a watersports centre.
On the opposite page there are descriptions of eight watersports centres.
Decide which centre would be the most suitable for the following people.
For questions **6–10**, mark the correct letter **(A–H)** on your answer sheet.

6

Victor and Olga need a personal instructor to teach them better powerboat skills, and to find their way safely around the waters off the coast. They want to go without booking in advance.

7

Felipe wants a weekend training session for his staff, to help them work well together. He'd like them to do sailing and indoor activities, and have comfortable overnight accommodation at the centre.

8

Harry wants to find a centre where top people in watersports train, and where he can measure his skills to see if he could compete professionally. However, he can't afford anything too expensive.

9

Tania and Paolo can already waterski, and want to try another challenging watersport. They want to go in the evenings, and be able to eat at the centre afterwards.

10

Laura and Adam want to celebrate Laura's birthday at a watersports centre with friends, some of whom prefer to do indoor sports. They'd like to have a good idea of what the place is like before going.

Watersports centres

A Fossey Centre

The Fossey Centre has indoor and outdoor activities. Arrange a session at the big lake, with watersports facilities good enough for even professionals to practise on, plus indoor football and tennis. No individual training is available. However, there's no need to book in advance as the Centre is rarely busy.

B Marinewater

The Marinewater website shows their whole range of watersports from sailing to the exciting experience of controlling a boat on a fast-moving river. The route is used by professional athletes in training, so it is lit until late, while the Centre's restaurant serves delicious meals. Booking is recommended.

C Blore Centre

If you're looking for somewhere to provide staff training, then the Blore Centre is perfect. There's a range of activities, with powerboats, sailing or an indoor sports centre – ideal for team-building. There's a campsite for overnight stays but it's extremely basic.

D Marston Centre

The Marston Centre offers courses at all levels for learning to manage every kind of boat you can think of. Fees for private teaching sessions are reasonable, and it isn't essential to arrange this before you go. The centre also offers training in how not to get lost at sea. See their website!

E Padcaster Centre

The huge lake at the Padcaster Centre is perfect for waterskiing and sailing. It's regularly used by sportspeople preparing for the Olympics, and has a cycle path around the outside for your coach to accompany you on land and check your speed. See how you compare with the champions! Prices are very fair.

F Camford Centre

The Camford Centre offers sailing for people who love relaxing on the water, and also has volleyball and badminton courts in its well-designed building. Check out their website – their 360-degree video tours show you exactly what's available. And if you're coming for a special occasion, tell us – we'll prepare a fantastic meal in our restaurant!

G Casson Centre

The Casson Centre and café are open all day until 9 pm. The Centre's professional staff offer individual training in sailing and waterskiing, for which booking is essential. The small hotel on site is useful for anyone travelling a long way to the Centre.

H Aqua Sports

Aqua Sports offers company team-building courses that can include water sports on the lake or a range of things to do in the gym. You can select the perfect timetable for your team. Afterwards, you can have a good night's sleep in the Centre's excellent hotel.

Part 3

Questions 11–20

Look at the sentences below about a motorbike trip.
Read the text on the opposite page to decide if each sentence is correct or incorrect.
If it is correct, mark **A** on your answer sheet.
If it is not correct, mark **B** on your answer sheet.

11   Graham says his friend Luke was keen for him to enjoy riding motorbikes.

12   Luke was confident their first ride with his club would be a totally positive experience.

13   For Graham's first group ride, they planned to go to a place 100 kilometres away.

14   One rider in their group, Tania, started her bike without help when it broke down.

15   Graham wondered if he would feel the same as Tania if his bike had the same problem.

16   At one point, the group leader decided to change the route they were following.

17   Luke was concerned that the weather conditions were making their ride dangerous.

18   They found that the clothes they were wearing protected them from the weather.

19   Luke and Graham's mood improved after they reached Graham's house.

20   Immediately after the trip Graham bought a new motorbike of his own.

My first long motorbiking trip – by Graham Jones

I began riding motorbikes when I was eighteen years old, as a passenger on the back of my friend Luke's bike. It was a classic motorbike – big, fast, and noisy! Our first few rides were short trips – which he was very careful to make as enjoyable as possible for me – and as a result I fell in love with the whole motorbike experience almost immediately.

After a couple of months of shorter rides, we went on a longer group ride with Luke's motorcycling club, which he said would give me a good idea of the pleasures and difficulties of motorcycling. We rode approximately 100 km in one day, and it was a great experience – although we only managed to get less than half of the way to our destination. The ride was wonderful and we had beautiful weather as we went along the quiet roads. However, after we'd stopped to have a rest and were about to carry on riding, one rider in the group, Tania, suddenly found her bike wouldn't start. Some people in the group finally managed to get it going, but in the end Tania had to turn round and go back home by herself, knowing that if she stopped anywhere, she wouldn't be able to start her bike again. She bravely decided she could ride back home alone, but I doubted whether I'd have such a confident attitude in the same situation.

Our group then drove on to the mountains and stopped for some lunch – and that's where things started to go wrong. The weather turned bad and it began to snow. Then, without asking anyone, the leader of the group had the idea of going in a completely new direction up a steep mountain road, with corners that would be difficult for motorbikes even when the weather was good – and by now it was snowing quite heavily!

When we finally made it to the top of the mountain, Luke was annoyed. He said it was too risky to be on a mountain in such bad weather, and that we should go back down. We were both frozen when we reached the bottom, despite our cold-weather clothes. However, when we got back to my house we both began to see the funnier side of it all, and I immediately asked Luke when we could go again. I realised I could handle the worst of times on a motorbike, and there and then I made up my mind to try and save up for one.

Part 4

Questions 21–25

Read the text and questions below.
For each question, mark the correct letter **A**, **B**, **C** or **D** on your answer sheet.

American Black Ducks

by Sam Prentice, wildlife biologist

I work at a US university where my team and I are trying to learn more about water birds, particularly one called the American black duck. And we've just started using an exciting piece of equipment called a 'night-vision scope', which allows us to see the ducks in the dark!

We're worried about black ducks mainly because their numbers have fallen hugely and we don't know whether there's enough food on the east coast for these animals. There's lots of information about their daytime activities, but nothing about what they do at night, because we simply haven't had the equipment. But this new 'scope' will produce really clear pictures, even on moonless nights, so we'll be able to find out more and make better decisions about looking after the area where they live based on what we learn.

It is very hard work. There are four of us, each working six hours daily. We've studied ducks in different locations, and I've had to take a boat to some sites and make notes on every duck I see. The weather hasn't helped – some nights are mild, but more often it's wet. Oh, and it's so quiet I've needed lots of coffee to stop me falling asleep! We've only missed one working day so far, because the snow was too deep even for our special snow vehicles.

Still I like the challenge of it, especially compared to what the summer will bring – hours in a laboratory, where we'll look at our results together. It'll be hard to be stuck inside – but it's essential to do this. And I wouldn't change it for anything!

21 What is Sam Prentice doing in the text?

    A   describing how he became a wildlife biologist

    B   explaining how he is doing a piece of research

    C   suggesting how readers can learn about one type of bird

    D   giving a report of success he's had in his work

22 What is Sam hoping to discover about American black ducks?

    A   what their behaviour is like after dark

    B   which kind of food they need to live on

    C   which animals are responsible for the fall in their numbers

    D   what makes the east coast a suitable location for them

23 When Sam spends long periods watching ducks, he

    A   dislikes having to deal with low temperatures.

    B   finds there's enough to do to maintain his interest.

    C   is glad of the chance to be in a quiet place.

    D   sometimes finds it difficult to stay awake.

24 What does Sam say about working inside a lab over the summer?

    A   He feels pleased that he'll avoid the hot weather.

    B   He accepts that it's a necessary part of his job.

    C   He's looking forward to studying his results.

    D   He's glad he'll be working with other people.

25 What might Sam say about his experiences of working outdoors?

    A   Having the right vehicle for bad weather has meant we've still carried on working, whatever it's been like outside.

    B   We decided that we'd only go to sites that were easy to get to, and I'm really glad we made that decision.

    C   Sometimes the moon hasn't been very bright, but our equipment provides the amount of light we need to collect information.

    D   The other people in my team are brilliant, but it's been hard watching ducks in the same place every day.

Part 5

Questions 26–35

Read the text below and choose the correct word for each space.
For each question, mark the correct letter **A**, **B**, **C** or **D** on your answer sheet.
Example:

0   **A** certain   **B** particular   **C** special   **D** suitable

Answer:
0	A B C D
	■ ▢ ▢ ▢

Wool

Wool comes from sheep and **(0)** .... other animals like goats and rabbits. Over a million tonnes of wool is produced every year, of **(26)** .... 60% goes into clothes. The wool that is used **(27)** .... comes from Australian Merino sheep. Their wool is good for baby clothes, as it is soft, **(28)** .... babies warm, and can **(29)** .... their bodies.

When wool is first cut from the sheep, it **(30)** .... a high level of a valuable oil, so before the wool is used, it must be cleaned. The **(31)** .... way to do this is by putting the wool in warm water. The oil that is **(32)** .... from the wool is widely used in products like hand creams.

Sheep were first used by humans several thousand years ago, **(33)** .... it is believed that this was for meat **(34)** .... than wool. When people developed a way of cutting the wool from sheep it **(35)** .... a more important material.

26	**A**	what	**B**	whose	**C**	which	**D**	that
27	**A**	mostly	**B**	nearly	**C**	properly	**D**	truly
28	**A**	stays	**B**	helps	**C**	rests	**D**	keeps
29	**A**	protect	**B**	wrap	**C**	care	**D**	save
30	**A**	involves	**B**	contains	**C**	receives	**D**	consists
31	**A**	simplest	**B**	clearest	**C**	plainest	**D**	nearest
32	**A**	carried	**B**	passed	**C**	removed	**D**	divided
33	**A**	while	**B**	but	**C**	or	**D**	because
34	**A**	rather	**B**	instead	**C**	apart	**D**	except
35	**A**	arrived	**B**	turned	**C**	grew	**D**	became

WRITING

Part 1

Questions 1–5

Here are some sentences about buying a sports car.
For each question, complete the second sentence so that it means the same as the first.
Use no more than three words.
Write only the missing words on your answer sheet.
You may use this page for any rough work.

Example:

0 Ben's old car stopped working so he needed to buy a new one.

Ben needed to buy a new car .... **his old one stopped working.**

Answer: | **0** | *because*

---

1   His friend Frieda suggested that Ben should buy a second-hand car.

‘**Why** .... **a second-hand car, Ben?’ suggested Frieda.**

2   Ben didn't have enough money for a new car.

Ben couldn't afford .... **buy a new car.**

3   Ben contacted the owner of a car for sale after seeing an advert.

Ben got in touch .... **the owner of a car for sale after seeing an advert.**

4   Ben drove the car and decided immediately that he liked it.

Ben decided he liked the car as .... **he drove it.**

5   The car was cheaper than Ben had expected.

The car was .... **expensive than Ben had expected.**

Part 2

Question 6

Your English friend, Alex, is coming to your town for the day, and wants to meet you.

Write an email to Alex. In your email, you should

- explain where you can meet
- suggest what you can do together
- advise Alex what to bring.

Write **35–45 words** on your answer sheet.

Visual material for the Speaking test

1B

2C

2A

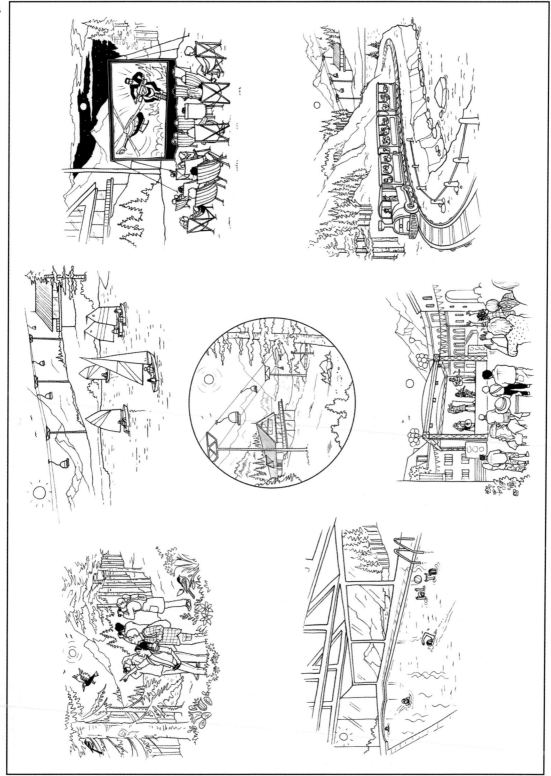

1C

4B

3A

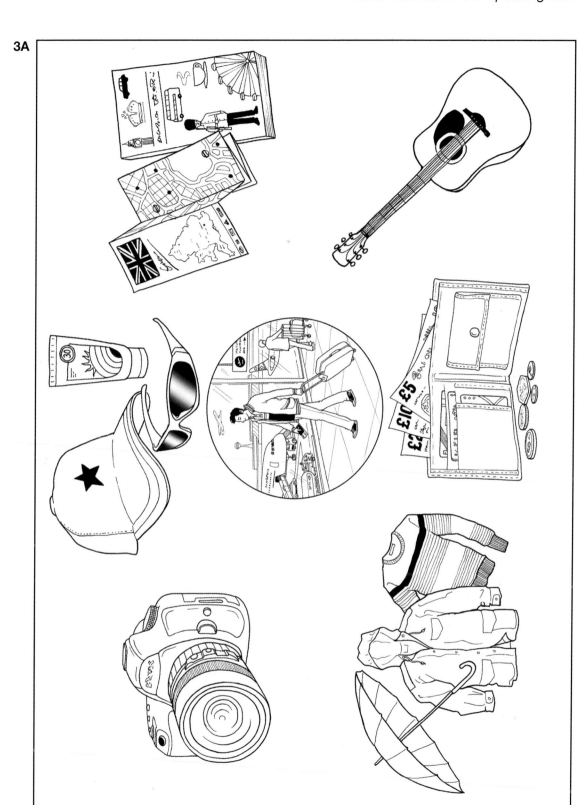

3B

4C

4A

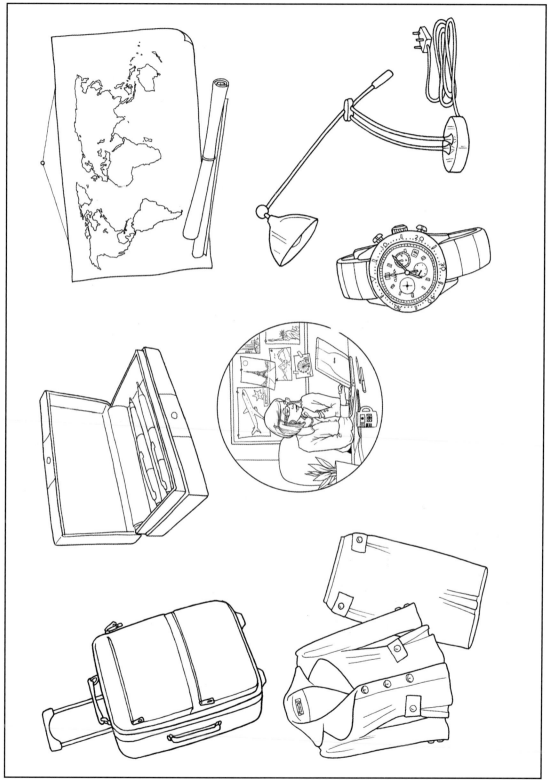

2B

3C

4D

Part 3

Write an answer to **one** of the questions (**7** or **8**) in this part.
Write your answer in about **100 words** on your answer sheet.
Tick the box (**Question 7** or **Question 8**) on your answer sheet to show which question you have answered.

Question 7

- This is part of a letter you receive from an English friend.

> I've won some prize money in a competition, and I'm not sure what to do. My family think I should save the money, but I want to spend it all on an exciting holiday. What should I do?

- Now write a letter to your friend, giving your advice.
- Write your **letter** in about 100 words on your answer sheet.

Question 8

- Your English teacher wants you to write a story.
- This is the title for your story:

The day I met my hero

- Write your **story** in about 100 words on your answer sheet.

PAPER 2   LISTENING   approx 35 minutes
(including 6 minutes transfer time)

Part 1

Questions 1–7

There are seven questions in this part.
For each question there are three pictures and a short recording.
Choose the correct picture and put a tick (✓) in the box below it.

Example: How did the woman hear about the wedding?

A ☑

B ☐

C ☐

---

1   How are they going to get to the café?

A ☑

B ☐

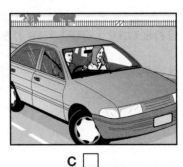

C ☐

2   What has the man had a problem with?

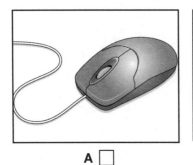

A ☐

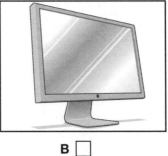

B ☐

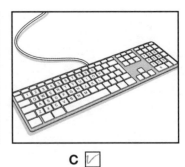

C ☑

3   When does the man plan to get up?

A ☐   B ☑   C ☐

4   What are they going to order?

A ☐   B ☐   C ☑

5   What is the woman phoning about?

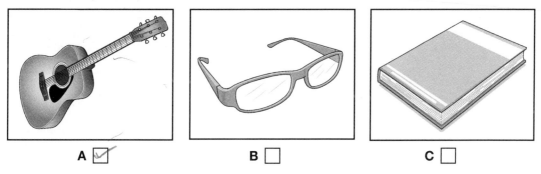

A ☑   B ☐   C ☐

6 What are they going to watch first?

A ☐   B ☐   C ☑

7 What is the woman going to buy?

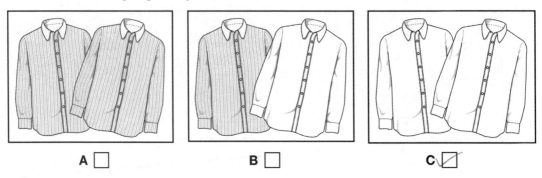

A ☐   B ☐   C ☑

Part 2

Questions 8–13

You will hear an interview with a young man called Jack Salter, who has won a photography competition.
For each question, put a tick (✓) in the correct box.

8	Why did Jack take photographs of street signs?	**A**	His mother suggested it.	☐
		B	The colours were exciting.	☐
		C	He liked their different shapes.	☐

9	Why did Jack go into his yard to take his winning photo?	**A**	He wanted to be out in the sunshine.	☐
		B	He was looking for shots of flowers.	☐
		C	He was trying out some new equipment.	☐

10	When Jack first looked at his winning photo, he felt	**A**	proud of how good it was.	☐
		B	worried about the background.	☐
		C	unsure how clear the detail was.	☐

11	Jack was surprised by the other photos in the competition because	**A**	the quality was so high.	☐
		B	the styles were so similar.	☐
		C	the subjects were so unusual.	☐

12 Since winning the competition, Jack now hopes to

    A take more photos of people. ☐

    B travel to different countries. ☑

    C get ideas from other photographers. ☐

13 Jack advises other young people interested in photography to

    A have the same attitude as him. ☑

    B photograph the same things as him. ☐

    C get the same type of camera as him. ☐

Part 3

Questions 14–19

You will hear some information about a student running club.
For each question, fill in the missing information in the numbered space.

STUDENT RUNNING CLUB

The club meets at the **(14)** .... in the town.

Last year's members will be sent a registration form by **(15)** ....

Members who pay $5 receive a special **(16)** .... that shows the club's name.

All runners will get a **(17)** .... as a free gift.

You know the runner's level of experience by the colour of their **(18)** ....

Contact Carol **(19)** .... on 8302195.

Part 4

Questions 20–25

Look at the six sentences for this part.
You will hear a woman called Anne and a man called Peter talking about a college party.
Decide if each sentence is correct or incorrect.
If it is correct, put a tick (✓) in the box under **A** for **YES**. If it is not correct, put a tick (✓) in the box under **B** for **NO**.

		A YES	B NO
20	Peter wants to take his sister to the party.	☑	☐
21	Anne hopes the party will be bigger than the one last year.	☐	☐
22	Peter thinks the new college hall is big enough for the party.	☐	☑
23	Peter thinks DJs play a good range of music.	☐	☑
24	Anne hopes the college cafeteria will supply the food for the party.	☐	☐
25	Peter is confident the party will end after midnight.	☑	☐

About the Speaking test

The Speaking test lasts about 10 to 12 minutes. You take the test with another candidate. There are two examiners in the room. One examiner talks to you and the other examiner listens to you. Both the examiners give you marks.

Part 1

The examiners introduce themselves and then one examiner asks you and your partner to say your names and spell them. This examiner then asks you questions about yourself, your daily life, interests, etc.

Part 2

The examiner asks you to talk about something together and gives you a drawing to help you.

Part 3

You each have a chance to talk by yourselves. The examiner gives you a colour photograph to look at and asks you to talk about it. When you have finished talking, the examiner gives your partner a different photograph to look at and to talk about.

Part 4

The examiner asks you and your partner to say more about the subject of the photographs in Part 3. You may be asked to give your opinion or to talk about something that has happened to you.

Test 4

PAPER 1   READING AND WRITING (1 hour 30 minutes)

READING

Part 1

Questions 1–5

Look at the text in each question. What does it say?
Mark the correct letter **A**, **B** or **C** on your answer sheet.

Example:

0

Special one-day drama class this Saturday.
Price – £50 per person.
Anyone who attends will be able to book our new six-week course at a discount.

A The six-week course is cheaper if you also do the one-day class.

B The one-day class is free for those who book the six-week course.

C You must pay for the six-week course before you do the one-day class.

Answer: 0 A B C

1

John
I've seen an advert for a new French restaurant in the town centre. Have you eaten there? Would it be suitable for Mum's birthday on Saturday?
Julie

A Julie is asking John if French food is available at a new restaurant.

B Julie is inviting John to a birthday party in the town centre.

C Julie wants John's advice about a venue for a family celebration

2

Olympia Sportswear

Further discounts available on certain sale items. Check label for details.

A Customers can get discounts on all goods in the sale.

B Customers can only get reduced prices on goods with labels.

C Customers can get special prices on some goods.

3

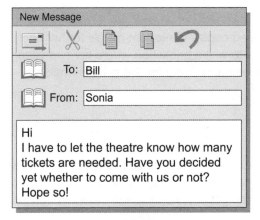

New Message

To: Bill

From: Sonia

Hi
I have to let the theatre know how many tickets are needed. Have you decided yet whether to come with us or not? Hope so!

Sonia has written the email to

A find out if Bill wants a theatre ticket.

B tell Bill how many theatre tickets they need.

C remind Bill to get some theatre tickets.

4

Matt
Sunday's race starts at 10.00. We can pick up our numbers at registration one hour before. There are no changing facilities so we must arrive ready to run.
Jo

A Jo wants Matt to pick her up an hour before the race starts.

B Jo is reminding Matt to put on his running kit before he leaves home.

C Jo is expecting Matt to collect their race numbers from registration before she arrives.

5

COMFORTABLE SOFA
£20
too large for my new apartment

Buyer must collect

Call Andre: 298354

A Andre wants to buy a large sofa for his new apartment.

B Andre will sell his sofa as long as it is taken away.

C Buyers should call Andre to arrange transport for the sofa.

Part 2

Questions 6–10

The people below are all looking for second-hand books.
On the opposite page there are descriptions of some second-hand bookshops.
Decide which bookshop would be the most suitable for the following people.
For questions **6–10**, mark the correct letter **(A–H)** on your answer sheet.

6

Yang is looking for used copies of modern novels for her book group. She would like to visit a bookshop where her two young daughters will be welcome, with drinks and snacks available.

7

Stefan loves beautiful art books but would like to check what's available on the Internet before visiting. He wants to find a bookshop where he can get lunch and spend the afternoon looking at books.

8

Scott has been unable to get a particular textbook which he needs urgently for his project on health care for the elderly. He is very busy and would prefer to have it delivered.

9

Jasmin is setting up a library of classic fiction for her primary school. Before buying some books online, she would like to go to the shop and discuss suitable books with staff.

10

Ian wants a quiet bookshop where he can relax in comfort with a coffee for a few hours after a long day at work. He'd like to get a few cheap novels to take home.

Second–hand bookshops

A Bookworm

This shop has used books for all tastes but customers will have to visit in person and look around as Bookworm does not have a website. The best sections are on medicine, cookery and art. These include some rare and expensive books.

B Bales

This shop is famous for its range of titles, from college textbooks to classic literature, and is known for its peaceful atmosphere. Regular customers come for the excellent café with its sofas and armchairs, which stays open until late.

C Westwood's

There's no room to sit down in this tiny back street bookshop, and the owner is often too busy to chat. On the first floor are children's books and fine art books for collectors. At entrance level there are less expensive general fiction hardbacks.

D Topping's

You'll only find good-quality used hardback books here on certain subjects. Topping's is run by three experts in art, travel and literature for the young. They are happy to chat and advise customers. The shelves are well-organised, and books can also be ordered from the shop's website.

E Scrimshaw's

Scrimshaw's has a huge selection of books showing the works of the great painters. Most are in excellent condition and reasonably priced, and the store's online guide is regularly updated. The basement also has a café and a large number of out-of-date school textbooks on sale.

F Regal

Here you'll find the country's largest selection of science-related books, including topics such as psychology and medicine. There are 70,000 used and new books, all at discount prices. Regal also has an efficient online ordering service plus comfortable sofas and freshly made coffee, and is open during office hours.

G Holt's

Although its prices are high, the fun of Holt's is its lively atmosphere. It's in an old railway station, where you can enjoy afternoon tea and cake in the waiting room. Or leave the kids to play in the former ticket office while you look at the huge selection of recent fiction.

H Wenlock's

This prize-winning bookshop is noted for its wide selection of titles, both paperback and hardback. Fiction is downstairs, non-fiction upstairs under the ancient roof of this 15th century building. The book club welcomes new members to discuss a different novel one evening each month.

Part 3

Questions 11–20

Look at the sentences below about an Arctic expedition.
Read the text on the opposite page to decide if each sentence is correct or incorrect.
If it is correct, mark **A** on your answer sheet.
If it is not correct, mark **B** on your answer sheet.

---

11   A building was ready for the scientists to work in on their arrival in northern Canada.

12   This was the first time scientists had tested Arctic sea water during the winter months.

13   Information was collected on the expedition to help explain the reasons for climate change.

14   The North Pole was the destination of a previous expedition that Ann had been on.

15   Ann had to do special training to be strong enough for the expedition.

16   During her career, Ann has discovered ways to deal with feeling cold.

17   Ann's group achieved everything they had aimed to do.

18   Helen knew it would be difficult doing experiments in freezing conditions.

19   When she went onto the ice, Helen carried equipment to prevent wild animals from attacking.

20   The expedition research is now available for other scientists to read.

Arctic expedition

Ann Daniels and Helen Findlay faced the dangers of polar bears, thin ice and frostbite when they became members of an expedition to the Arctic in 2010.

The expedition team consisted of six scientists and a separate group of three explorers. While Helen and the other scientists were setting up a laboratory site on the ice in northern Canada, Ann and two other explorers set off on a 500 kilometre journey on foot across floating sea ice from Greenland to the North Pole.

Both groups planned to measure how thick the ice was at various sites in the Arctic. They would also collect water samples for testing, in order to discover how the chemistry of sea water was changing, and what effect this was having on plant-life and animals in the ocean. On previous expeditions, the water was tested in the summer, using ships at sea, but they had never collected it from under the ice before. The research was important for understanding what might happen in other oceans around the world in the future, as a result of climate change.

Ann Daniels was working in a bank in 1996 when she answered an advert, inviting ordinary women to join a trek to the North Pole in the Arctic. Since then she has become one of the world's leading professional polar explorers. For the 2010 expedition, she and her two colleagues attended a week-long fitness camp to prepare them for pulling the 120 kilogram sledges over the ice for 12 hours a day.

Despite her previous experience, however, Ann suffered in the freezing conditions. 'It gets into your bones and never leaves you, even when you're in your tent at night,' she said. 'Especially at the end of an expedition when you're totally exhausted.' Yet Ann successfully guided her companions for 73 days and collected all the samples and information that were needed.

Helen Findlay was one of the scientists on the laboratory site based in Canada. Although it was not her first visit to the Arctic, she had never been there in winter and realised that carrying out experiments in such an extreme environment would be challenging. The laboratory tents were heated, but getting equipment to work outside while wearing gloves and thick clothes meant every job took twice as long as it would normally. When they went out onto the ice to collect samples, the scientists were protected by two guides with guns and bangers to frighten any curious polar bears who might be attracted by the smell of humans.

Despite the difficulties, both Ann and Helen stayed out on the ice for the whole of the project, and the results of their studies have been widely published.

Part 4

Questions 21–25

Read the text and questions below.
For each question, mark the correct letter **A**, **B**, **C** or **D** on your answer sheet.

Helen Skelton

Television presenter Helen Skelton has completed various dangerous challenges for charity, including a desert marathon run and a journey down the Amazon river in a tiny boat. For her latest challenge, Helen walked on a high wire, a long thin piece of metal, 66 metres above the ground, between the two towers of an empty power station. There was no safety net, only a belt around her waist attached to another wire above. To help her keep her balance and not to fall, she carried a long stick, weighing eight kilograms.

Helen took lessons from an expert high-wire walker. Although she already had a few circus skills, she quickly discovered that high-wire walking was completely different. 'The training was a shock', said Helen. 'I didn't realise how strong I'd need to be. Every day started at 8 am with a run up a steep hill; then came an hour of exercises, with another hour of them after my day practising on the wire. I also had to learn how to fall onto the wire so that if I slipped I could carry on. Every time I fell on the wire it hurt badly. But it was essential to keep a positive attitude: if I was nervous and started shaking, so would the wire!'

The day of the actual challenge was windy and Helen controlled herself by taking deep breaths as she moved step by step along the wire. The 150-metre walk took 15 minutes. 'That was the scariest thing I've done,' she admitted afterwards. 'I'm glad it's over!'

The experience has not prevented Helen, however, from planning her next charity project: to reach the South Pole by ski, kite and bike.

21   What is the writer doing in this text?
    A   introducing a new television presenter
    B   getting support for a charity project
    C   describing a woman's achievement
    D   recommending a television programme

22 Helen knew she would be safe if she fell because

    A   she had a net that could catch her.

    B   she had a stick to support herself with.

    C   she was wearing special equipment.

    D   she was quite close to the ground.

23 During her training, Helen was surprised to find that

    A   staying on the wire was so difficult.

    B   she had to work so hard at her fitness.

    C   it was so important to be confident.

    D   her circus skills were so useful.

24 When Helen performed her work on the high wire

    A   she was sorry to get to the end.

    B   the weather conditions were perfect.

    C   it took less time than expected.

    D   she managed to keep herself calm.

25 What might Helen say about the walk?

A

> The view from the high wire was fantastic – I loved every minute of it. I can't wait to have another go.

B

> I must admit I was a little bit frightened, but it wasn't nearly as bad as going down the Amazon on my own.

C

> That was the longest quarter of an hour of my life. I couldn't breathe at all when I first stepped onto the wire.

D

> The training could be painful at times but at least I'm in really good condition now, ready for my next challenge.

Part 5

Questions 26–35

Read the text below and choose the correct word for each space.
For each question, mark the correct letter **A**, **B**, **C** or **D** on your answer sheet.

Example:

0	**A** agree	**B** decide	**C** approve	**D** inform

Answer:

0	A B C D
	▬ ▢ ▢ ▢

Finding Gold

Most people would **(0)** .... that finding the perfect ring for your partner is difficult. However, John Greenwood, a Scottish engineer, **(26)** .... himself an extra challenge. **(27)** .... of taking a trip to the jeweller's, John **(28)** .... much of last year standing up to his knees in freezing water. He was looking for tiny pieces of gold **(29)** .... the stones on the river beds in the Scottish Highlands.

Using very **(30)** .... equipment, John worked hard to **(31)** .... enough gold to make not just an engagement ring for his girlfriend, Morag, **(32)** .... also their two wedding rings. 'I was out there **(33)** .... weekend and in the evenings before it got dark, in freezing cold water,' he said.

Experts think that John was amazingly lucky to find so much gold in such a **(34)** .... time. Many people **(35)** .... for 30 years without getting anything.

26	**A** did	**B** made	**C** gave	**D** had
27	**A** Rather	**B** Besides	**C** Along	**D** Instead
28	**A** took	**B** paid	**C** spent	**D** held
29	**A** among	**B** towards	**C** against	**D** through
30	**A** easy	**B** plain	**C** necessary	**D** basic
31	**A** choose	**B** collect	**C** pick	**D** select
32	**A** or	**B** and	**C** but	**D** even
33	**A** every	**B** some	**C** most	**D** any
34	**A** little	**B** short	**C** quick	**D** small
35	**A** reach	**B** follow	**C** search	**D** keep

WRITING

Part 1

Questions 1–5

Here are some sentences about a train journey.
For each question, complete the second sentence so that it means the same as the first.
Use no more than three words.
Write only the missing words on your answer sheet.
You may use this page for any rough work.

Example:

0 The train journey from London to York takes about two hours.

It takes about two hours .... **travel from London to York by train.**

Answer:

0	*to*

---

1 It was several months since Jessica last went on a train.

Jessica hadn't been on a train .... **several months.**

2 Jessica bought her ticket in advance online.

Jessica's ticket .... **bought in advance online.**

3 It wasn't easy to find a seat because the train was crowded.

The train was .... **crowded that it was difficult to find a seat.**

4 Jessica asked what time they would arrive in York.

Jessica asked 'What time .... **we arrive in York?'**

5 The journey wasn't boring for Jessica because she had a good book.

Jessica .... **find the journey boring because she had
a good book.**

Part 2

Question 6

You and your friend, Jerry, have tickets for a football match at the weekend, but now you cannot go.

Write a note to Jerry. In your note, you should

- apologise to Jerry
- explain why you cannot go
- suggest what Jerry could do with your ticket.

Write **35–45 words** on your answer sheet.

Part 3

Write an answer to **one** of the questions (**7** or **8**) in this part.
Write your answer in about **100 words** on your answer sheet.
Tick the box (**Question 7** or **Question 8**) on your answer sheet to show which question you have
answered.

Question 7

• This is part of a letter you receive from a friend.

> I can't decide whether to buy a new bicycle from a
> shop or on the Internet. Where do you think I
> should buy it? Is it better to buy some things from
> shops? Do you buy things on the Internet?

• Now write a letter answering your friend's questions.
• Write your **letter** in about 100 words on your answer sheet.

Question 8

• Your English teacher has asked you to write a story.
• Your story must begin with this sentence:

I was amazed when I opened the bag.

• Write your **story** in about 100 words on your answer sheet.

PAPER 2   LISTENING   approx 35 minutes
(including 6 minutes transfer time)

Part 1

Questions 1–7

There are seven questions in this part.
For each question there are three pictures and a short recording.
Choose the correct picture and put a tick (✓) in the box below it.

Example: Where did the man leave his camera?

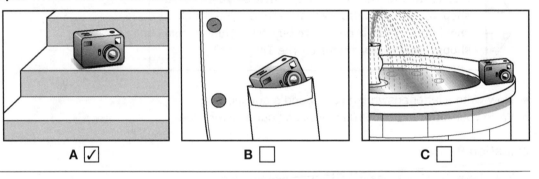

A ✓   B ☐   C ☐

---

1   Where will Peter give Joanna the book?

A ☐   B ☐   C ☐

2   What did the girl buy at the market?

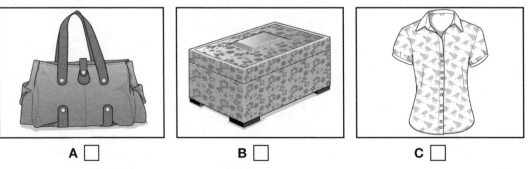

A ☐   B ☐   C ☐

3   What will the weather be like for the race?

A ☐   B ☐   C ☐

4   What does the girl like best about the city?

A ☐   B ☐   C ☐

5   What does the boy think was unusual about the film?

A ☐   B ☐   C ☐

6   What happened during the football match?

A ☐   B ☐   C ☐

7   Which part of the gallery did the man visit?

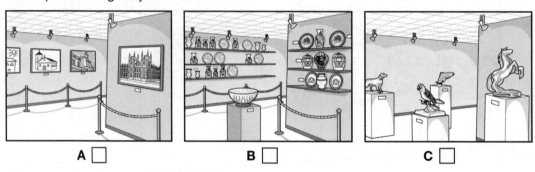

A ☐   B ☐   C ☐

Part 2

Questions 8–13

You will hear an interview with a woman called Amy Rowntree, who works as a fashion designer.
For each question, put a tick (✓) in the correct box.

8	Amy decided to become a fashion designer while	**A**	she was still at school.	☐
		B	she was working in a shop.	☐
		C	she was helping run a fashion show.	☐

9	Amy says the most important skill for a designer is	**A**	remaining patient in difficult situations.	☐
		B	knowing about different materials.	☐
		C	understanding how clothes are made.	☐

10	What does Amy particularly like about her work?	**A**	being able to sell her designs	☐
		B	seeing her clothes on display	☐
		C	having her name recognised	☐

11	How does Amy feel about today's fashion?	**A**	She would like clothes to be more practical.	☐
		B	She feels clothes should be more attractive.	☐
		C	She's pleased sports clothes are popular.	☐

12 What helps Amy find new ideas for designs?

   A seeing things around her. ☐

   B going to visit museums. ☐

   C looking at photos of clothes. ☐

13 What project is Amy working on at the moment?

   A a collection of clothes for a film ☐

   B a fashion show in New York ☐

   C a new range for a London store ☐

Part 3

Questions 14–19

You will hear a student called Steve talking about working in a forest in New Zealand.
For each question, fill in the missing information in the numbered space.

Working in a forest in New Zealand

Steve had accommodation in a shared **(14)** ....

Steve says it was important to have good **(15)** .... at the end of each day.

Steve worked with a team that made a **(16)** .... through the forest.

Steve also collected information needed for a **(17)** .... of the forest area.

In the morning Steve was surprised to hear the sound of **(18)** .... in the forest.

When he did the trip, Steve only had to pay for his **(19)** ....

Part 4

Questions 20–25

Look at the six sentences for this part.
You will hear a woman called Martha and a man called James talking about a TV series called *Madison*, which is about a doctor who works in a hospital.
Decide if each sentence is correct or incorrect.
If it is correct, put a tick (✓) in the box under **A** for **YES**. If it is not correct, put a tick (✓) in the box under **B** for **NO**.

		A YES	B NO
20	They agree that the last show in the series was complicated	☐	☐
21	James believes that the series is successful because of the main character.	☐	☐
22	They both admire the main character's behaviour.	☐	☐
23	Martha thinks that the main character has similar skills to a detective.	☐	☐
24	James was surprised to find the main character so funny.	☐	☐
25	They both plan to watch the series again.	☐	☐

About the Speaking test

The Speaking test lasts about 10 to 12 minutes. You take the test with another candidate. There are two examiners in the room. One examiner talks to you and the other examiner listens to you. Both the examiners give you marks.

Part 1

The examiners introduce themselves and then one examiner asks you and your partner to say your names and spell them. This examiner then asks you questions about yourself, your daily life, interests, etc.

Part 2

The examiner asks you to talk about something together and gives you a drawing to help you.

Part 3

You each have a chance to talk by yourselves. The examiner gives you a colour photograph to look at and asks you to talk about it. When you have finished talking, the examiner gives your partner a different photograph to look at and to talk about.

Part 4

The examiner asks you and your partner to say more about the subject of the photographs in Part 3. You may be asked to give your opinion or to talk about something that has happened to you.

Frames for the Speaking test

TEST 1

Part 1 (2–3 minutes)

Tasks   Identifying oneself; giving information about oneself; talking about interests.

Phase 1
Examiner

A/B	Good morning / afternoon / evening. Can I have your mark sheets, please?
A/B	I'm .... and this is .... He / she is just going to listen to us.
A	Now, what's your name? Thank you.
B	And what's your name? Thank you.

Back-up prompts

B	Candidate B, what's your surname? How do you spell it? Thank you.	How do you write your family / second name?
A	And, Candidate A, what's your surname? How do you spell it? Thank you.	How do you write your family / second name?

(Ask the following questions. Use candidates' names throughout. Ask Candidate A first.) Where do you live / come from? <u>Adult students</u> Do you work or are you a student in . . .? What do you do / study? <u>School-age students</u> Do you study English at school? Do you like it? Thank you. *(Repeat for Candidate B.)*	Do you live in . . .? Have you got a job? What job do you do? / What subject(s) do you study? Do you have English lessons?

Phase 2
Examiner

(Select one or more questions from the list to ask each candidate. Ask Candidate B first.)

	Back-up prompts
Do you enjoy studying English? Why (not)?	Do you like studying English?
Do you think that English will be useful for you in the future?	Will you use English in the future?
What did you do yesterday evening / last weekend?	Did you do anything yesterday evening / last weekend? What?
What do you enjoy doing in your free time?	What do you like to do in your free time?

Thank you.

(Introduction to Part 2)

In the next part, you are going to talk to each other.

Part 2 (2–3 minutes)

UNIVERSITY SPORTS CENTRE

Tasks   Discussing alternatives; expressing opinions; making choices.

Examiner   *Say to both candidates:*

> I'm going to describe a situation to you.
>
> A university is going to build a **new sports centre** for students. Talk together about the different sports the students could do in the sports centre and say which would be most **popular**.
>
> Here is a picture with some ideas to help you.

Ask both candidates to look at picture 1A on page I of the Student's Book and repeat the frame.

> I'll say that again.
>
> A university is going to build a **new sports centre** for students. Talk together about the different sports the students could do in the sports centre and say which would be most **popular**.
>
> All right? Talk together.

Allow the candidates enough time to complete the task without intervention. Prompt only if necessary.

Part 3 (3 minutes)

PEOPLE AND FOOD

Tasks	Describing people and places; saying where people and things are and what different people are doing.
Examiner	*Say to both candidates:*

> Now, I'd like each of you to talk on your own about something. I'm going to give each of you a photograph of **people** and **food**.
>
> Candidate A, here is your photograph. *(Ask Candidate A to look at photo 1B on page II of the Student's Book.)* Please show it to Candidate B, but I'd like you to talk about it. Candidate B, you just listen. I'll give you your photograph in a moment.
>
> Candidate A, please tell us what you can see in the photograph.

(Candidate A)	*Approximately one minute.*
	If there is a need to intervene, prompts rather than direct questions should be used.
	Ask Candidate A to close his / her book.
Examiner	Now, Candidate B, here is your photograph. It also shows **people** and **food**. *(Ask Candidate B to look at photo 1C on page IV of the Student's Book.)* Please show it to Candidate A and tell us what you can see in the photograph.
(Candidate B)	*Approximately one minute.*
	Ask the candidates to close their books before moving to Part 4.

Part 4 (3 minutes)

Tasks	Talking about one's likes and dislikes; expressing opinions.
Examiner	*Say to both candidates:*

> Your photographs showed **people** and **food**. Now I'd like you to talk together about the food **you** like and say **where** you usually eat.

Allow the candidates enough time to complete the task without intervention. Prompt only if necessary.

> **Back-up prompts**
> 1 Talk about the food **you** like.
> 2 Talk about **where** you usually eat.
> 3 Talk about where you can **buy** food in your area.
> 4 Talk about how **often** you **cook**.

> Thank you. That's the end of the test.

TEST 2

Part 1 (2–3 minutes)

Tasks   Identifying oneself; giving information about oneself; talking about interests.

Phase 1
Examiner

A/B	Good morning / afternoon / evening. Can I have your mark sheets, please?
A/B	I'm ………… and this is ………… . He / she is just going to listen to us.
A	Now, what's your name? Thank you.
B	And what's your name? Thank you.

Back-up prompts

B	Candidate B, what's your surname? How do you spell it? Thank you.	How do you write your family / second name?
A	And, Candidate A, what's your surname? How do you spell it? Thank you.	How do you write your family / second name?

(Ask the following questions. Use candidates' names throughout. Ask Candidate A first.) Where do you live / come from? *Adult students* Do you work or are you a student in . . .? What do you do / study? *School-age students* Do you study English at school? Do you like it? Thank you. *(Repeat for Candidate B.)*	Do you live in . . .? Have you got a job? What job do you do? / What subject(s) do you study? Do you have English lessons?

Phase 2
Examiner

(Select one or more questions from the list to ask each candidate. Ask Candidate B first.)

	Back-up prompts
Do you enjoy studying English? Why (not)?	Do you like studying English?
Do you think that English will be useful for you in the future?	Will you use English in the future?
What did you do yesterday evening / last weekend?	Did you do anything yesterday evening / last weekend? What?
What do you enjoy doing in your free time?	What do you like to do in your free time?

Thank you.

(Introduction to Part 2)

In the next part, you are going to talk to each other.

Part 2 (2–3 minutes)

SKI RESORT IN SUMMER

Tasks   Discussing alternatives; expressing opinions; making choices.

Examiner   *Say to both candidates:*

> I'm going to describe a situation to you.
>
> A small **ski** resort wants to attract **more visitors** in the **summer**. Talk together about the different things the ski resort could have to attract more visitors in the summer and say which would be most **popular**.
>
> Here is a picture with some ideas to help you.

Ask both candidates to look at picture 2A on page III of the Student's Book and repeat the frame.

> I'll say that again.
>
> A small **ski** resort wants to attract **more visitors** in the **summer**. Talk together about the different things the ski resort could have to attract more visitors in the summer and say which would be most **popular**.
>
> All right? Talk together.

Allow the candidates enough time to complete the task without intervention Prompt only if necessary.

Part 3 (3 minutes)

PEOPLE SPENDING TIME WITH FRIENDS

Tasks   Describing people and places; saying where people and things are and what
                   different people are doing.

Examiner   *Say to both candidates:*

Now, I'd like each of you to talk on your own about something. I'm going to give
each of you a photograph of **people spending time with friends**.

Candidate A, here is your photograph. *(Ask Candidate A to look at photo 2B on page
VIII of the Student's Book.)* Please show it to Candidate B, but I'd like you to talk
about it. Candidate B, you just listen. I'll give you your photograph in a moment.

Candidate A, please tell us what you can see in the photograph.

(Candidate A)   *Approximately one minute.*

If there is a need to intervene, prompts rather than direct questions should be used.

Ask Candidate A to close his / her book.

Examiner   Now, Candidate B, here is your photograph. It also shows **people spending
                   time with friends**. *(Ask Candidate B to look at photo 2C on page II of the
                   Student's Book.)* Please show it to Candidate A and tell us what you can see in
                   the photograph.

(Candidate B)   *Approximately one minute.*

Ask the candidates to close their books before moving to Part 4.

Part 4 (3 minutes)

Tasks   Talking about one's likes and dislikes; expressing opinions.

Examiner   *Say to both candidates:*

Your photographs showed **people spending time with friends**. Now I'd like you
to talk together about when **you** spend time with **your** friends and say what you
like **doing** together.

Allow the candidates enough time to complete the task without intervention.
Prompt only if necessary.

Back-up prompts

1   Talk about when **you** spend time with
    your friends.
2   Talk about **what** you like **doing** with
    your friends.

Thank you. That's the end
of the test.

3   Talk about things you did with your
    friends when you were **younger**.
4   Talk about some **new** things you and
    your friends would like to do together.

TEST 3

Part 1 (2–3 minutes)

Tasks   Identifying oneself; giving information about oneself; talking about interests.

Phase 1
Examiner

A/B	Good morning / afternoon / evening. Can I have your mark sheets, please?
A/B	I'm .... and this is .... He / she is just going to listen to us.
A	Now, what's your name? Thank you.
B	And what's your name? Thank you.

Back-up prompts

B	Candidate B, what's your surname? How do you spell it? Thank you.
A	And, Candidate A, what's your surname? How do you spell it? Thank you.

How do you write your
family / second name?

How do you write your
family / second name?

*(Ask the following questions. Use
candidates' names throughout.
Ask Candidate A first.)*

Where do you live / come from?

Do you live in . . .?

<u>Adult students</u>
Do you work or are you a student in . . .?
What do you do / study?

Have you got a job?
What job do you do? / What
subject(s) do you study?

<u>School-age students</u>
Do you study English at school?
Do you like it?

Do you have English lessons?

Thank you.

(Repeat for Candidate B.)

Phase 2
Examiner

(Select one or more questions from the list to ask each candidate. Ask Candidate B first.)

Do you enjoy studying English? Why (not)?	Do you like studying English?
Do you think that English will be useful for you in the future?	Will you use English in the future?
What did you do yesterday evening / last weekend?	Did you do anything yesterday evening / last weekend? What?
What do you enjoy doing in your free time?	What do you like to do in your free time?

Thank you.

(Introduction to Part 2)

In the next part, you are going to talk to each other.

Part 2 (2–3 minutes)

SUMMER JOB

Tasks   Discussing alternatives; expressing opinions; making choices.

Examiner   *Say to both candidates:*

> I'm going to describe a situation to you.
>
> A young man is going to travel to **England** to do a **summer job**. Talk together about the different things he should take with him and say which would be most **useful**.
>
> Here is a picture with some ideas to help you.

Ask both candidates to look at picture 3A on page V of the Student's Book and repeat the frame.

> I'll say that again.
>
> A young man is going to travel to **England** to do a **summer job**. Talk together about the different things he should take with him and say which would be most **useful**.
>
> All right? Talk together.

Allow the candidates enough time to complete the task without intervention. Prompt only if necessary.

Frames for the Speaking test

Part 3 (3 minutes)

DOING THINGS OUTSIDE

Tasks	Describing people and places; saying where people and things are and what different people are doing.
Examiner	*Say to both candidates:*

> Now, I'd like each of you to talk on your own about something. I'm going to give each of you a photograph of **people doing things outside**.
>
> Candidate A, here is your photograph. *(Ask Candidate A to look at photo 3B on page VI of the Student's Book.)* Please show it to Candidate B, but I'd like you to talk about it. Candidate B, you just listen. I'll give you your photograph in a moment.
>
> Candidate A, please tell us what you can see in the photograph.

(Candidate A) *Approximately one minute.*

If there is a need to intervene, prompts rather than direct questions should be used.

Ask Candidate A to close his / her book.

Examiner

> Now, Candidate B, here is your photograph. It also shows **people doing things outside**. *(Ask Candidate B to look at photo 3C on page VIII of the Student's Book.)* Please show it to Candidate A and tell us what you can see in the photograph.

(Candidate B) *Approximately one minute.*

Ask the candidates to close their books before moving to Part 4.

Part 4 (3 minutes)

DOING THINGS OUTSIDE

Tasks	Talking about one's likes and dislikes; expressing opinions.
Examiner	*Say to both candidates:*

> Your photographs showed **people doing things outside**. Now I'd like you to talk together about the things **you** like **doing** outside and what you enjoy **watching** outside.

Allow the candidates enough time to complete the task without intervention. Prompt only if necessary.

Back-up prompts

1. Talk about the things **you** like **doing** outside.
2. Talk about what you enjoy **watching** outside.
3. Talk about doing things outside in **winter/ summer**.
4. Talk about **outdoor activities** you would like to **try**.

> Thank you. That's the end of the test.

TEST 4

Part 1 (2–3 minutes)

Tasks   Identifying oneself; giving information about oneself; talking about interests.

Phase 1
Examiner

A/B   Good morning / afternoon / evening.
Can I have your mark sheets, please?

A/B   I'm ………… and this is ………… .
He / she is just going to listen to us.

A   Now, what's your name?
Thank you.

B   And what's your name?
Thank you.

Back-up prompts

B
| Candidate B, what's your surname? |
| How do you spell it? |
| Thank you. |

How do you write your
family / second name?

A
| And, Candidate A, what's your surname? |
| How do you spell it? |
| Thank you. |

How do you write your
family / second name?

(Ask the following questions. Use candidates' names throughout. Ask Candidate A first.)

Where do you live / come from?

Adult students
Do you work or are you a student in . . .?
What do you do / study?

School-age students
Do you study English at school?
Do you like it?

Thank you.

(Repeat for Candidate B.)

Do you live in . . .?

Have you got a job?
What job do you do? / What subject(s) do you study?

Do you have English lessons?

Phase 2
Examiner

(Select one or more questions from the list to ask each candidate. Ask Candidate B first.)

Back-up prompts

Do you enjoy studying English? Why (not)?	Do you like studying English?
Do you think that English will be useful for you in the future?	Will you use English in the future?
What did you do yesterday evening / last weekend?	Did you do anything yesterday evening / last weekend? What?
What do you enjoy doing in your free time?	What do you like to do in your free time?
Thank you.	

(Introduction to Part 2)

In the next part, you are going to talk to each other.

Part 2 (2–3 minutes)

FIRST JOB (SUITABLE FOR GROUPS OF THREE AND PAIRS)

Tasks   Discussing alternatives; expressing opinions; making choices.

Examiner   *Say to both / all candidates:*

> I'm going to describe a situation to you.
>
> A young woman has just started her **first job**, working for a **travel magazine**. Her parents want to give her a **present**. Talk together about the different things they could give her and say which would be **best**.
>
> Here is a picture with some ideas to help you.

Ask both / all candidates to look at picture 4A on page VII of the Student's Book and repeat the frame.

> I'll say that again.
>
> A young woman has just started her **first job**, working for a **travel magazine**. Her parents want to give her a **present**. Talk together about the different things they could give her and say which would be **best**.
>
> All right? Talk together.

Allow the candidates enough time to complete the task without intervention. Prompt only if necessary.

Part 3 (3–4 minutes)

SHOPPING (SUITABLE FOR GROUPS OF THREE AND PAIRS)

Tasks	Describing people and places; saying where people and things are and what different people are doing.
Examiner	*Say to both / all candidates:*

> Now, I'd like each of you to talk on your own about something. I'm going to give each of you a photograph of **people shopping**.
>
> Candidate A, here is your photograph. *(Ask Candidate A to look at photo 4B on page IV of the Student's Book.)* Please show it to Candidate(s) B (and C), but I'd like you to talk about it. Candidate(s) B (and C), you just listen. I'll give you your photograph(s) in a moment.
>
> Candidate A, please tell us what you can see in the photograph.

(Candidate A)	*Approximately one minute.*
	If there is a need to intervene, prompts rather than direct questions should be used.
	Ask Candidate A to close his / her book.
Examiner	

> Now, Candidate B, here is your photograph. It also shows **people shopping**. *(Ask Candidate B to look at photo 4C on page VI of the Student's Book.)* Please show it to Candidate(s) A (and C) and tell us what you can see in the photograph.

(Candidate B)	*Approximately one minute.*
	Ask Candidate B to close his / her book.
Examiner	

> Now, Candidate C, here is your photograph. It also shows **people shopping**. *(Ask Candidate C to look at photo 4D on page VIII of the Student's Book.)* Please show it to Candidates A and B and tell us what you can see in the photograph.

(Candidate C)	*Approximately one minute.*
	Ask the candidates to close their books before moving to Part 4.

Part 4 (3–4 minutes)

Tasks	Talking about one's likes and dislikes; expressing opinions.
Examiner	*Say to both / all candidates:*

> Your photographs showed **people shopping**. Now, I'd like you to talk together about where **you** like shopping and the **things** you like to **buy**.

Allow the candidates enough time to complete the task without intervention. *Prompt only if necessary.*	**Back-up prompts**
	1 Talk about where **you** like shopping.
	2 Talk about the **things** you like to **buy**.
	3 Talk about **who** you like shopping **with**.
Thank you. That's the end of the test.	4 Talk about **what** you would like to buy if you had **a lot of money**

Key

Test 1

PAPER 1 READING AND WRITING

READING

Part 1

1 C   2 A   3 B   4 B   5 A

Part 2

6 B   7 H   8 D   9 E   10 G

Part 3

11 A   12 A   13 B   14 A   15 A   16 B   17 B   18 A   19 B   20 B

Part 4

21 B   22 D   23 B   24 A   25 C

Part 5

26 B   27 A   28 C   29 D   30 A   31 C   32 B   33 C   34 B   35 A

WRITING

Part 1

1 gave   2 first time   3 how   4 well as   5 forward

Part 2 & 3

The following sample answers can be used as a guide when marking.

SAMPLE A (Test 1, Question 6: Email to a friend)

> Hey Robin! I missed you last Friday! Why didn't you come when we arranged to meet? I felt disappointed with you but I hope you have a good explanation.
>
> What if we meet on Monday 8, at 18.00 p.m?
>
> Waiting for your answer,
>
> Mery

Examiner Comments

All three parts of the message are clearly communicated.

Mark: 5

SAMPLE B (Test 1, Question 6: Email to a friend)

> Hy! Why didn't you come? I wait for about two hours, I felt horrible because I want to have fun whit you and you didn't come, but mow I am fine. If you can, we will met Sunday at 3.00 o'clock.
>
> Goodbye

Examiner Comments

All three parts of the message are communicated but there are some non-impeding errors in spelling and grammar.

Mark: 4

SAMPLE C (Test 1, Question 6: Email to a friend)

Dear Robin

I wait to go on shoping with you. I like the first magazine on the street, number one. Your's taken tanen ijury beautiful. I'm buying a new shoes and new pencil. I have a one hundred (100) dalas.

Yours faithfully

Tony

Examiner Comments

There is some relevant content to points 2 and 3 but the errors in expression require patience and interpretation by the reader and impede communication.

Mark: 2

SAMPLE D (Test 1, Question 7: Letter to a friend)

> I enjoy everything about reading I think it's a good way to learn new things and still have fun. It's more relaxing to read than to play games on computer. I'd rather read a book than a magazine. I my country lived many well-known writer. But Mihai Eminescu was the best. He wrote poems, which are appreciate even nowadays. All of his poems have a deep messages, so not everyone can understand them. As you like reading, I think you should dome of his poems. I promise, you won't be disappointed.

Subscale	Mark	Examiner Comments
Content	5	All the content is relevant to the task. The target reader is fully informed.
Communicative Achievement	5	Register is appropriate although letter format has not been used. The ideas are communicated effectively and the target reader's attention is held throughout.
Organisation	4	The text is connected and coherent, using limited basic linking (*and; so*) and some cohesive devices (*it's a good way to learn; Mihai Eminescu was the best; He wrote poems which are; All of his poems*).
Language	5	A good range of everyday vocabulary is used and there is some less common lexis (*relaxing; well-known; appreciate*). A range of simple and some complex grammatical forms are used (*it's more relaxing to read than to play games on the computer; I'd rather read a book than a magazine; so that not everyone can understand them*). There are some errors but they do not impede communication.

SAMPLE E (Test 1, Question 7: Letter to a friend)

Hi Peter

I like very much your letter. I would like that you give me this book, for read it. I pefer read books than magazines. I love the romantic books because I like this beautiful historys about a man and a woman who are in love. And I hate the monster's books because this aren't real

My favourite writer of my country is Fernando de Rojos and I think his best book is "La Celestina", this is a very famous book. If you want I can give it to you

See you soon

Maria Isobel

Subscale	Mark	Examiner Comments
Content	5	All the content is relevant to the task. The target reader is fully informed.
Communicative Achievement	3	The conventions of the communicative task (appropriate register and letter format) are used in generally appropriate ways to communicate straightforward ideas. The target reader is able to follow most of the message without difficulty but there is some distraction, for example in the second paragraph.
Organisation	3	The text is connected and coherent and uses limited basic linking (*because*; *and*) and cohesive devices (*this beautiful historys*; *a man and woman who are in love*; *his best book*; *this is a very famous book*).
Language	3	Everyday vocabulary is used appropriately. Simple grammatical forms are used with a good degree of control and more complex grammatical forms are attempted but not always successfully (*I would like that you give me this book for read it*; *And I hate the monster's books because this aren't real*). Errors are noticeable but they are non-impeding.

SAMPLE F (Test 1, Question 7: Letter to a friend)

> Dear Holly
>
> Now me too, I have just finished reading a magnific book. This book is my best book and I read this book a few times.
> In my case, the kinds of my goods readings are romantic, comedy and horror.
>
> At this moment I prefer to read books but the magazines are the same important of books, because you know some information that you have not know.
>
> At the moment there are not any famous writer in my country but one year ago come JK Rowling, the writer of Harry Potter. It was so good. I want you some news
>
> See you soon

Subscale	Mark	Examiner Comments
Content	4	All the content is relevant but the second content point is confused. The target reader is on the whole informed.
Communicative Achievement	2	The conventions of the communicative task are used in generally appropriate ways (appropriate register and letter format). The target reader has to work very hard to follow the message, particularly in the second and third paragraphs and the high error frequency is distracting.
Organisation	2	There are limited basic linking words (*and*; *but*; *because*) and cohesive devices (*This book*; *In my case*; *At this moment*; *one year ago*). Paragraphing is used but not always successfully and the text lacks coherence.
Language	1	Everyday vocabulary is used appropriately but there is an overuse of certain lexis (*This book is my best book and I read this book … to read books … the same important of books*). Simple grammatical forms are used with a reasonable degree of control (*It was so good*). Complex grammatical forms are attempted but there are serious errors which sometimes impede communication (*the kinds of my goods readings are*; *because you know some information that you have not know*; *I want you some news*).

SAMPLE G (Test 1, Question 8: Story)

It was a sunny day, when Bilbo was taking his lunch. He had in mind to continue his book. He thought that it will be just a regular day in the shire. But suddenly someone knocked at the door. Bilbo opened the door and seen an old man, with grey long beard and grey clothes. He was wearing a witch hat, and he had a sceptre im his hands. Bilbo didn't know who that mam is, but he found out that he is a wizard named Gandalf. He proposed Bilbo an unexpected journey. Bilbo accepted and they went through moumtains.

Subscale	Mark	Examiner Comments
Content	5	The story follows on from the prompt sentence and the target reader is able to follow the storyline with no problems.
Communicative Achievement	4	Register and story format are appropriate. Ideas are generally communicated clearly, although some effort is required in the penultimate sentence.
Organisation	5	The text is generally well organised and coherent. There is limited basic linking (*But*; *and*) and a variety of cohesive devices are used (*a sunny day when*; *He thought that it will be*; *who that man is*; *he found out that he is*).
Language	5	Everyday vocabulary is used appropriately, and there is some less common lexis (*continue*; *sceptre*; *proposed*; *accepted*). A range of simple and some complex grammatical forms is used with a good degree of control (*He had in mind to continue*; *just a regular day in the shire*; *went through mountains*). Errors do not impede communication.

SAMPLE H (Test 1, Question 8: Story)

Last year, the 3ʳᵈ of July, my friends and I were in the beach playing with the water and splashing one to each other, and sudenly arrived our parents and told us that we had to go because my uncles phoned that they came here for some days and my mum had to prepare the beds, some meal for lunch and dinner and so on.

I was very ungry, because I was enjoying a lot with my friends but I could not do anything, but infarct later I enjoyed also a lot with my uncles because we played with the "Wii". And my friends and I meet other day.

Subscale	Mark	Examiner Comments
Content	5	The story is clearly related to the title. The target reader is fully informed.
Communicative Achievement	3	The conventions of the communicative task (appropriate register and story format) are used in generally appropriate ways and straightforward ideas are communicated. The target reader would have to work in places to follow the storyline.
Organisation	2	The text is linked using mostly basic linking (*and*; *because*; *but*) and consists mainly of two very lengthy sentences. The absence of appropriate punctuation and the overuse of the basic linking word *and* in the first paragraph make it difficult for the reader. There are limited cohesive devices (*Last year*; *told us that we had to go*; *later*).
Language	2	Everyday vocabulary is used generally appropriately. Simple grammatical forms are used with a reasonable degree of control. Complex grammatical forms are attempted but there are noticeable errors throughout the text (*splashing one to each other*; *my uncles phoned that they came here*; *my friends and I meet other day*; *ungry*; *I enjoyed also a lot with my uncles*; *infarct*).

SAMPLE I (Test 1, Question 8: Story)

> Once apon a time there was a king that lived in a big, white castle. The King, Ricardo, and the queen, Regina, had a litter dotter called Mery. Mery was a fantastic girl she played the piona, she song very well and she was an adventure girl. one day she was playing with her silver ball near the lake she throw the ball very tall, and the ball wend into the dip lake. Mery started to cry – what I'm going to do know? – she thought. Then a green unexpected visitor gave her the ball and disapere.

Subscale	Mark	Examiner Comments
Content	3	The story is loosely related to the title and there is not much information about the 'unexpected visitor'. The target reader is on the whole informed.
Communicative Achievement	2	The conventions of the communicative task (appropriate register and story format) are used to communicate mostly simple ideas in simple ways. The target reader can follow the story line with only a little effort.
Organisation	2	The text is connected and mostly coherent, using the basic linking word *and* and a limited number of cohesive devices (*Once upon a time there was a king that lived*; *a little dotter called Mery*: *one day*).
Language	2	In general, everyday vocabulary is used appropriately but there are some noticeable and distracting spelling errors (*dotter*; *fantastic*; *dip lake*; *disapere*). Mostly, simple grammatical forms are used with a reasonable degree of control. There are some difficulties with verb formation (*she song very well*; *she throw the ball*).

PAPER 2   LISTENING

Part 1

1 B   2 C   3 B   4 A   5 C   6 A   7 B

Part 2

8 C   9 A   10 A   11 B   12 C   13 B

Part 3

14 1 / one hour / hr 30 / thirty (minutes)
15 oil
16 (desert) plants
17 (large) (colourful) rocks
18 souvenirs
19 basket

Part 4

20 B   21 B   22 A   23 A   24 B   25 A

Key

Test 1 transcript

This is the Cambridge English: Preliminary, Test 1.

There are four parts to the test. You will hear each part twice. For each part of the test there will be time for you to look through the questions and time for you to check your answers.

Write your answers on the question paper. You will have six minutes at the end of the test to copy your answers onto the answer sheet.

The recording will now be stopped. Please ask any questions now, because you must not speak during the test.

[Pause]

Now open your question paper and look at Part 1.

PART 1 *There are seven questions in this part. For each question there are three pictures and a short recording. Choose the correct picture and put a tick in the box below it.*

Before we start, here is an example.

Where did the man leave his camera?

Man: Oh no! I haven't got my camera!

Woman: But you used it just now to take a photograph of the fountain.

Man: Oh I remember, I put it down on the steps while I put my coat on.

Woman: Well, let's drive back quickly – it might still be there.

[Pause]

The first picture is correct so there is a tick in box A.

Look at the three pictures for question 1 now.

[Pause]

Now we are ready to start. Listen carefully. You will hear each recording twice.

One. What did the man buy?

Woman: Hi, did you buy a new suit yesterday?

Man: Well, I went to the shopping centre, but I had no idea how expensive suits are.

Woman: I told you it would cost you a lot to buy one.

Man: I know. Anyway, I saw lots of nice shirts and stuff I liked.

Woman: But you've already got loads of shirts. You don't really need any more.

Man: Actually, I ended up with a rather stylish new sweater. When I've saved enough to buy a suit, we'd better go shopping together.

[Pause]

Now listen again.

[The recording is repeated]

[Pause]

Two. How will the woman help the man?

Man: Hi, Clara – just the person! Look, I'm giving a dinner party for my parents' wedding anniversary and might need a bit of help.

Woman: I'm not surprised. You can't cook, can you? All you buy is ready-meals from the supermarket.

Man: I know, but I'm going to get everything online from a company that cooks and delivers food to your home. I just want some help with choosing some dishes from their menu.

Woman: That sounds fun. Can I also choose a nice dessert? So, am I invited to the party?

Man: Of course.

116

[Pause]

Now listen again.

[The recording is repeated]

[Pause]

Three. What will the students buy for their teacher?

Man: We need to decide what to get as a present for Anne at the end of our course.

Woman: Yes, she's such a great teacher ... how about chocolates?

Man: That's not very exciting. We could get something to wear, like a scarf?

Woman: She seems to have loads of those already. What about flowers? She often says how much she loves flowers.

Man: But she told us she had a garden full of them! Let's go with your original idea and buy her the largest box possible!

[Pause]

Now listen again.

[The recording is repeated]

[Pause]

Four. Which exhibition is the busiest today?

Man: We haven't got much time left now. There's still so much to see in this museum.

Woman: We'll just have to choose one more exhibition. Can I have a look at the plan?

Man: What about Jewellery from the Ancient World?

Woman: But look at the queue. We'll spend half our time waiting if we go in there. Why not try The Rainforest in Photos? You can wander round and see all the forest animals.

Man: OK – then we won't have time to visit Rescue by Helicopter. There's a real one in there.

Woman: Maybe next time.

[Pause]

Now listen again.

[The recording is repeated]

[Pause]

Five. Where can visitors see the ducks?

Man: Hi everyone, and welcome to City Wildlife Park. I'll explain where things are and then you're free to go wherever you want. In front of us are some empty cages where the rabbits live. They're free to run about in the long grass, but come back to their cages when they're hungry! If you're interested in ducks, surprisingly they're not right here in the pond, but over there in one of their favourite places, near the dustbins. And we keep goats in the field here, together with some sheep.

[Pause]

Now listen again.

[The recording is repeated]

[Pause]

Six. What will the weather be like when the festival starts?

Woman: And now for the weather forecast for this Saturday and Sunday. People heading to the music festival starting on Saturday on the south coast should be prepared for different conditions over the next two days. Saturday will bring bright sunshine but cool temperatures for this time of year. Over night, however, clouds are expected to move in and Sunday will see dull skies bringing a further drop in temperatures, and there will be a good chance of rain later on.

Now listen again.

[The recording is repeated]

[Pause]

Seven. What has the man sent back to the company?

Man:	Hello. My name's John Masters. This is a message for the person I spoke to yesterday in Customer Services. You asked me to return the iron I bought from you in its box. I've done this, although as I mentioned to you the box was badly damaged when it arrived. Anyway, that's not the problem and the iron didn't look damaged at all. But when I switched it on, it didn't heat up. My order reference is 01376XB. I hope you'll replace the iron as soon as possible. Thank you.

[Pause]

Now listen again.

[The recording is repeated]

[Pause]

That is the end of Part 1.

[Pause]

PART 2   *Now turn to Part 2, questions 8 to 13.*

You will hear an interview with a man called Tim Jones, who organises an international summer course for young musicians.

For each question, put a tick in the correct box.

You now have 45 seconds to look at the questions for Part 2.

[Pause]

Now we are ready to start. Listen carefully. You will hear the recording twice.

Woman:	My guest today is Tim Jones, who organises an international summer course for young musicians. Tim, tell us all about it.
Tim:	Well, I'm lucky to have such a great job. Basically, young musicians come from all over the world and learn to play together as an orchestra. By the end of the six-week course, they're really good and hearing them play is what gives me most pleasure. Unfortunately, I don't get to know them all that well, as organising every single detail of the course keeps me busy.
Woman:	So, how do you find the young musicians?
Tim:	We advertise on the Internet. Anyone between the ages of sixteen and twenty can complete the application form and email it to us, along with a short recording of their playing. We're not looking for perfect performances or the stars of tomorrow – just people good enough to play in an orchestra. The course is in English, but only a basic level of spoken language is necessary.
Woman:	And the teachers?
Tim:	The teachers are well-known musicians. Because they want to help young people, they do this work for a very low salary, which is very kind of them. But it's my job to take care of them and make sure they're happy with their accommodation and so on. They generally have a great time, but some of them can be a bit difficult and sometimes complain about things.
Woman:	So where is the course held?
Tim:	In different places each year, actually, but it's usually a university during the summer holidays. They have large halls for practising, plus plenty of bedrooms and dining-rooms. Most importantly, though, the place has to have good rail, road and air connections, so somewhere in the middle of the countryside's no good.

Woman:	Do the students bring their own instruments?
Tim:	Mostly, yes. So, another thing to consider is security. Storing instruments in a locked room when they're not being used is essential. Can you imagine a hundred or more musical instruments lying around – violins, trumpets, flutes, cellos – all worth a lot of money. It would be terrible if one got damaged, or even worse stolen!
Woman:	And at the end of the course, there's a concert tour.
Tim:	That's right. I book concert halls and work out the programmes months in advance. It's important to get it right. Ticket prices aren't high, because we're not a professional orchestra, but lots of people buy them. We don't make a profit, but take enough money to pay for the students' travel and living expenses. It's a fantastic experience for them.

[Pause]

Now listen again.

[The recording is repeated]

[Pause]

That is the end of Part 2.

[Pause]

PART 3 *Now turn to Part 3, questions 14 to 19.*

You will hear an announcement about a train trip through a desert.

For each question, fill in the missing information in the numbered space.

You now have 20 seconds to look at Part 3.

[Pause]

Now we are ready to start. Listen carefully. You will hear the recording twice.

Man:	Hi everyone, I'd like to welcome you aboard our train trip through high desert scenery. The train that you are sitting in was built in 1933, so it's really old – but very comfortable! Our trip today lasts one-and-a-half hours and we will travel at a speed of about fifteen miles an hour. The train climbs uphill for the first forty-five minutes and then makes its way down to a town called Oldsville.
	In the twentieth century, oil was discovered here and an important industry developed. It didn't last long, however, and tourism is the biggest industry these days. There's lots to see in the town.
	On the journey you won't see any animals during the daytime because it's too hot, but you should look out for beautiful desert plants right next to the track, although at this height there are no trees.
	At one point, we go over an old wooden bridge. People get worried because it's noisy, but it's quite safe. There's no river under the bridge, but you can see some large colourful rocks – they're fantastic.
	We don't make any stops on the trip because all the stations were closed long ago. The route is kept open by local people who love the history of the railway and at the far end of our coach there's a small store. This store is really special and sells souvenirs which you can't buy anywhere else.
	The other things which we sell during your ride are drinks and snacks. Unfortunately, the machine selling these is broken, so once we're underway I'll be walking down the coach with everything in a basket. So stop me if you want anything.
	Enjoy your trip!

[Pause]

Now listen again.

[The recording is repeated]

[Pause]

That is the end of Part 3.

[Pause]

PART 4   *Now turn to Part 4, questions 20 to 25.*

Look at the six sentences for this part. You will hear a woman called Julie and a man called Greg talking about an indoor wildlife centre they have visited.

Decide if each sentence is correct or incorrect. If it is correct, put a tick in the box under A for YES. If it is not correct, put a tick in the box under B for NO.

You now have 20 seconds to look at the questions for Part 4.

[Pause]

Now we are ready to start. Listen carefully. You will hear the recording twice.

Greg: Hi Julie. Wasn't the indoor wildlife centre fantastic? I've never seen such an amazing building, with its glass walls and all those different floors.

Julie: Hi Greg. Didn't you find it tiring though, walking up so many stairs, and it was so hard to find your way round? That's not what I call good design.

Greg: I didn't really think about that.

Julie: It was an interesting start down in the basement, where it was so dark that I didn't see the sharks at first in the water behind the glass.

Greg: They were quite scary. You must know how dangerous they are.

Julie: Only if you're silly enough to swim with them! Anyway, what did you think of the temperature in the building?

Greg: It has to be so high in there because of all those tropical trees growing. They need a lot of heat.

Julie: I suppose so. It felt really uncomfortable to me. I loved the banana trees though.

Greg: Those butterflies right at the top of the building were amazing – so huge and colourful. But I thought there would be a lot more insects to see. There were hardly any really.

Julie: Just as well! Who wants to see a load of insects! I don't find them especially interesting at the best of times. Did you manage to see any tree frogs? They're so cute.

Greg: I spent ages hunting for them. They manage to hide by having skin that looks like part of a tree and they lie still without moving. I couldn't find a single one.

Julie: Yeah, they're not stupid – making sure they can't be seen by hungry birds! I really can't wait to go back 'cos there was just too much to see.

Greg: I'd like to read more about the wildlife before I think of going back there. Don't you think we'd enjoy it more if we knew more about the animals?

Julie: I'm not so sure really.

         [Pause]

         Now listen again.

         [The recording is repeated]

         [Pause]

         That is the end of Part 4.

         [Pause]

         You now have six minutes to check and copy your answers on to the answer sheet.

         Note: Teacher, stop the recording here and time six minutes. Remind students when there is **one** minute remaining.

         That is the end of the test.

Test 2

PAPER 1 READING AND WRITING

READING

Part 1

1 B   2 B   3 C   4 C   5 A

Part 2

6 E   7 B   8 H   9 C   10 F

Part 3

11 B   12 B   13 A   14 B   15 A   16 A   17 B   18 A   19 A   20 B

Part 4

21 C   22 B   23 A   24 D   25 D

Part 5

26 D   27 A   28 C   29 B   30 C   31 D   32 B   33 C   34 C   35 A

WRITING

Part 1

1 goes / comes
2 better / more
3 since
4 until
5 such

Part 2 & 3

The following sample answers can be used as a guide when marking.

Test 2

SAMPLE A (Test 2, Question 6: Postcard to a friend)

> Hi Sam
>
> I'm in Guetaria, a wonderful place in the Basque Country. I chose this place because a friend of mine recommended it. I like it because is a very small town, with a lots of restaurants and a beautiful beach. The most I enjoyed is a trip in a boat to fish. While we were fishing a terrible storm started with terrible thunders.
>
> I will return next saturday and I would be happy to meet you to give you sume gifts I've bought for you.
>
> Best regards.

Examiner Comments

All three parts of the message are clearly communicated.

Mark: 5

SAMPLE B (Test 2, Question 6: Postcard to a friend)

> Dear Sam,
>
> I'm in Cadiz spending a few days. I have chosen this town because my mother recommended me and it is raally bautiful! I have enjoyed a lot going to the beach and swimming in the sea! The water had a nice temperature.
>
> I hope we could meet when I get back!
>
> Love,
>
> Marta

Examiner Comments

Points 1 and 2 are clearly communicated. Point 3 is attempted but remains unclear.

Mark: 4

SAMPLE C (Test 2, Question 6: Postcard to a friend)

Dear Sam

I'm writing to you in St Florent, while the sun is coming, and the view is magnific I like the wild coast, beaches and high mountains. It's well worth a visit I've been climbing very high hills and when I arrived at the town I've been swimming on the beach. Although I don't want tp come back next week I'll be there, so, we could meet in Central Park on Friday if you want.

See you later

Idoia

Examiner Comments

Point 1 is not attempted. Points 2 and 3 are clearly communicated.

Mark: 3

SAMPLE D (Test 2, Question 7: Letter to a friend)

Hello, I just recieved your letter where you asked about popular films in my country. In Ukraine people like films with explosions and blood, but I don't like these films. I like comedies, adventure films for example Indiana Johns, A Journey to the centre of the Earth. There are a lot of funny and interesting moments. I know a good film, Red Heat, with Arnold Swarzeneger, and Moon Lightning with Bruce Willis – it's a detective film. You should watch all these films because they all are interesting and please recomend it to your friends.

Best wishes Vava

Subscale	Mark	Examiner Comments
Content	4	The candidate has addressed both task points with some expansion but has given information about more than one film. The target reader is not fully informed about the second point.
Communicative Achievement	5	The conventions of the communicative task are used to hold the target reader's attention. The text is in suitable letter format and appropriate register throughout. Straightforward ideas are communicated effectively.
Organisation	5	The text is connected and coherent using a variety of basic linking words (*but*; *and*; *because*) and cohesive devices (*your letter where*; *these films*; *for example*; *it's a detective film*; *all these films*).
Language	5	A range of everyday vocabulary appropriately used with some less common lexis (*explosions*; *comedies*; *detective film*). There is a range of simple and some complex grammatical forms with a good degree of control (*I don't like these films*; *I know a good film, Red Heat with Arnold Swarzeneger*; *You should watch all these because they are all interesting*). There are a few minor errors which do not impede communication (*recieved*; *recomend*).

SAMPLE E (Test 2, Question 7: Letter to a friend)

Dear Leila,

Hi, how it's going? I'm happy that you in film club now. In your last letter you wanted me to suggest you a good film from our country. Well I don't really like films from our country but treres a one film I really like. It's name is ,,Russian Roulette" It's about a girl who come to Poker Club and play Poker. But the one thing, she don't know how to play. After a few games she won lot's of money. She go to Las Vagas and become popular as ,,Russian Roulette girl" I like this film because actors play very good and it's very interesting. Well that's all for now. I hope I answered all your questions. I want you to write me about your favourite film.

Anastasia

Subscale	Mark	Examiner Comments
Content	3	The content is relevant to the task but the candidate has not addressed the first task point. The target reader is informed on the whole.
Communicative Achievement	4	Uses the conventions of the communicative task (appropriate register and an attempt at letter format) to communicate straightforward ideas.
Organisation	4	The text is generally well organised and coherent. Basic linking words (*but*; *and*; *because*) and some cohesive devices (*you wanted me to suggest to you*; *Well*; *a girl who come to Poker Club*) but the range is quite limited. The lack of paragraphing makes it more difficult for the reader.
Language	2	Basic vocabulary and some less common words (*Russian Roulette*; *favourite*) are used appropriately and spelling is accurate. Simple grammatical forms are used with some degree of control but there are a number of distracting errors which obscure the message (*to suggest you*; *a girl who come to Poker Club and play Poker*; *she don't know how to play*; *become popular*; *actors play very good*).

Key

SAMPLE F (Test 2, Question 7: Letter to a friend)

> Hello Megan
>
> I'm very glad to know about you and your new experience with the club. I don't understand too much about films but I'll try to help you. Some people like terrorific films but I don't.
>
> My friends tend to see american films, but I tend to see short films, and really, I don't think there are interesting in all for your club. But there's a very peculiar one, wich hasn't got music or speaking, "Hierro 3", of japonian director. It's like a poem in the cinema.
>
> I hope you will enjoy with it
>
> All the best
>
> Idoia

Subscale	Mark	Examiner Comments
Content	5	All the content is relevant to the task. The target reader is fully informed.
Communicative Achievement	3	The conventions of the communicative task (appropriate register and letter format) are used in generally appropriate ways and the target reader's attention is mostly held. There is some distraction in the middle of the second paragraph.
Organisation	3	The text is connected and coherent, using basic linking (*and*; *but* (which is overused)) and a number of cohesive devices (*I'll try to help you*; *Some people*; *a very peculiar one*; *I hope you will enjoy it*).
Language	3	Everyday vocabulary is used generally appropriately and there is some less common lexis (*tend to*; *poem*). Simple grammatical forms are used with a reasonable degree of control (*wich hasn't got music or speaking*). There are some noticeable errors throughout (*terrorific*; *wich*) some of which impede (*there are interesting in all for your club*; *of japonian director*).

SAMPLE G (Test 2, Question 8: Story)

> I was seven years old. My parents wanted to go somewhere abroad.
> They choosed Italian bus tour. We packed all our items and started
> our travel. Later we arrived to the capital of Italia. There were many
> beautiful houses and palaces. We visited famous museums, we also
> went to very interesting excursions, which told us about a history
> of Italia The Italian nature was beautiful, too. Several days later we
> visited another city. I was very upset when the journey ended.
>
> I'll never forget bus tour. I hope I'll visit Italia soon too.

Subscale	Mark	Examiner Comments
Content	5	All content is relevant to the task. The target reader is fully informed and would be able to follow the storyline with no problems.
Communicative Achievement	5	Straightforward ideas are communicated effectively following the conventions of storytelling and the register and format are appropriate. The target reader's attention is held throughout.
Organisation	5	The text is generally well organised. The narrative is connected and coherent, using limited basic linking words (*and*) and a variety of cohesive devices (*Later; also; which; several days later; I was very upset when the journey ended*).
Language	4	A range of everyday vocabulary used appropriately and some less common lexis (*somewhere abroad; the capital of Italia; palaces; museums; interesting excursions*). Simple and some complex grammatical forms are used with a good degree of control but there are a few distracting errors (*They choosed; arrived to; went to very interesting excursions; a history of Italia*).

SAMPLE H (Test 2, Question 8: Story)

> When I was 10 my friend and I decided to travell by bus. We wanted to go to London. We took our clothes and stopped to wait for our bus. We were waiting for it 1 hour and when it arrived it was dark outside. While we were sleep the bus stopped and small girl come into the bus. We woke up and looked at her strangely. She wore a white dress and red boots. We were skared because her eyes were all in blood and she carried a knife in her hands. After a few second she stopped the bus and go out. We screamed. The bus driver turned around and asked what happend. We told him about girld but he didn't believe us. This story I will never forget.

Subscale	Mark	Examiner Comments
Content	5	All content is relevant to the task and the target reader is fully informed and would have no problem following the story.
Communicative Achievement	5	Ideas are communicated effectively following the conventions of storytelling. Register and format are consistently appropriate and the target reader's attention is held.
Organisation	4	The text is generally well organised and coherent. There is a limited number of basic linking words with the repeated use of *and*, and some cohesive devices including good use of referencing pronouns (*we were waiting for it … when it arrived*; *We woke up and looked at her*; *After a few second*; *We told him about girld but he didn't believe us*).
Language	4	There is a range of everyday vocabulary used appropriately. Mostly simple and some complex grammatical forms are used with a good degree of control (*looked at her strangely*; *decided to travell*; *she carried a knife in her hands*). There are a few distracting errors (*we were sleep*; *we were skared*; *her eyes were all in blood*) but these do not impede communication.

SAMPLE I (Test 2, Question 8: Story)

> When I was 15 years old, my parents and I decided to go on holidays to a town in Extremadura called Miajadas.
>
> It was summer and it was very hot, so they decided to start our journey early in the morning. When we arraived to Madrid, we got into a big traffic jam and we were stoped in the road for 3 hours. After that, we continued our journey, but when we were arriving to Miajadas, our bus broke down. We had to wait for 2 hours until a van cames and took the bus to a garage.
>
> Finally, at 11 o'clock in the night, we arrived to the town in a taxi. I will never forget this journey!

Subscale	Mark	Examiner Comments
Content	5	All the content is relevant to the title and the story is easy to follow. The target reader is fully informed.
Communicative Achievement	4	The story format is appropriate and a suitable register is used consistently. Straightforward ideas are communicated and the target reader's attention is mostly held but minor errors cause some distraction (*arraived to Madrid*; *until a van cames*; *11o'clock in the night*).
Organisation	3	The text is connected and coherent, using basic linking words (*and*; *so*; *when*; *but*) and a limited number of cohesive devices (*After that*; *Finally*).
Language	3	Everyday vocabulary is used appropriately and some less common words (*early*; *big traffic jam*; *continued*). Simple grammatical forms are used with a good degree of control. There are some noticeable errors, particularly in the formation of verbs (*arraived to*; *we were stoped*; *when we were arriving to Miajadas*).

Key

Part 1
1 B   2 C   3 C   4 A   5 A   6 B   7 A

Part 2
8 B   9 A   10 C   11 C   12 C   13 B

Part 3
14 hills
15 sunset
16 cushion
17 5 / five
18 picnic
19 CITYENTS

Part 4
20 B   21 B   22 B   23 A   24 A   25 A

Test 2 transcript

This is the Cambridge English: Preliminary, Test 2.

There are four parts to the test. You will hear each part twice. For each part of the test there will be time for you to look through the questions and time for you to check your answers.

Write your answers on the question paper. You will have six minutes at the end of the test to copy your answers onto the answer sheet.

The recording will now be stopped.

Please ask any questions now, because you must not speak during the test.

[Pause]

Now open your question paper and look at Part 1.

[Pause]

There are seven questions in this part. For each question there are three pictures and a short recording. Choose the correct picture and put a tick in the box below it.

Before we start, here is an example.

Where did the man leave his camera?

Man: Oh no! I haven't got my camera!

Woman: But you used it just now to take a photograph of the fountain.

Man: Oh I remember, I put it down on the steps while I put my coat on.

Woman: Well, let's drive back quickly – it might still be there.

[Pause]

The first picture is correct so there is a tick in box A.

Look at the three pictures for question 1 now.

[Pause]

Now we are ready to start. Listen carefully. You will hear each recording twice.

One. Which part of the Arts Centre only opened recently?

Woman: In the heart of the city the Arts Centre includes a concert hall, cinema and an art gallery. The cinema is presenting a programme of films by younger film-makers and is attracting larger audiences than ever. The open-air concert area is the new home to the City Orchestra with an exciting concert programme of new composers and guest performers, while the City Art Gallery has a major programme of exhibitions all summer. Guests can enjoy dinner in the popular restaurant and enjoy the wonderful views of the city and river.

[Pause]

Now listen again.

[The recording is repeated]

[Pause]

Two. What does the shop assistant give the man?

Man: Excuse me, I bought this sweater here, but when I got home I noticed it had a hole in it.

Woman: Oh, I'm sorry. Oh yes, I see. Well I can certainly exchange it for you. We have plenty more – or would you like your money back instead?

Man: Well, I'd actually prefer one of those shirts over there but you haven't got my size. Oh, don't worry about it. I'll just have a refund, please.

Woman: Of course. We're having more shirts in next week if you're interested.

[Pause]

Now listen again.

[The recording is repeated]

[Pause]

Three. Where does the woman feel pain?

Woman: Hello, it's Maria here. Just to let you know about my health problems again. I saw Dr Jones last week about my knee and he told me to rest. It still hurts and he said if things don't improve, I should go back and see him again. Honestly, it was my ankle a few weeks ago. At least my headaches seem to have gone for the moment. Give me a ring and let me know how you are. Let's meet for a coffee soon. Call me back.

[Pause]

Now listen again.

[The recording is repeated]

[Pause]

Four. Where must the woman go to buy dollars?

Man: Can I help you?

Woman: I'd like to buy some dollars, please.

Man: Do you bank with us? We only sell dollars to customers who have an account at this bank.

Woman: No, I'm a tourist – I'm just in the country for a few days. I just wanted to change some euros into dollars. What do you suggest I do then?

Man: There's a currency exchange office at the airport.

Woman: That's so far away! Is there nowhere nearer? In a shopping mall, for example?

Man: Sorry, there used to be an exchange office in the big department store in the mall, but it closed last year.

[Pause]

Now listen again.

[The recording is repeated]

[Pause]

Five. Which vegetable is used in all today's recipes?

Man: On today's Student Cookery programme, I'm going to show you how to make some really cheap and healthy meals. Forget about opening tins and think fresh! You can do wonderful things with tomatoes, potatoes – and I don't mean chips or fries! – even cabbage, yes cabbage rolls, filled with tasty rice and herbs. And the essential vegetable in all my recipes is the ordinary onion, red or white or brown – colour doesn't matter. First of all, you need a sharp knife. So, watch carefully and off we go ...

[Pause]

Now listen again.

[The recording is repeated]

[Pause]

Six. Where is the meeting?

Man: Do you know where today's meeting with the Theatre Director will be held?

Woman: I thought it was in his office. Let me check his online diary.

Man: He did say he might hold it outdoors as it's so hot. But that's never a very good idea as papers can get blown away. I hope it's in the staff restaurant – I could do with a cold drink!

Woman: Ah, here it is in the diary – he's arranged it down by the lake. You could take something to drink with you – enjoy!

[Pause]

Now listen again.

[The recording is repeated]

[Pause]

Seven. How did the man want to pay?

Man: You'd think that paying a bill would be easy. On tonight's *Money Today*, I'm looking at some of the difficulties there can be. The story starts with my own experience. Thinking it'd be simpler, I made the mistake of trying to pay a hotel bill in cash. Well, amazingly they insisted on me using a credit card. I didn't have one with me, so had to get onto my internet banking site using my mobile phone to try and get my card details. Nothing's easy.

[Pause]

Now listen again.

[The recording is repeated]

[Pause]

That is the end of Part 1.

[Pause]

PART 2 *Now turn to Part 2, questions 8 to 13.*

You will hear an interview with a woman called Marta Stanston, who runs a mobile restaurant that she sets up in different places.

For each question, put a tick in the correct box.

You now have 45 seconds to look at the questions for Part 2.

[Pause]

Now we are ready to start. Listen carefully. You will hear the recording twice.

Man: Today I'm talking to Marta Stanston, who runs her own 'mobile' restaurant. Marta, how did you get into the restaurant business?

Marta: Well, I learnt to cook at college. I always wanted to open my own restaurant – but had no money. So I got a job as a chef. I had all sorts of ideas for new dishes, which the staff thought would sell, but the guy who owned the place wasn't interested. That's when a friend told me about the 'mobile restaurant' idea. It sounded great.

Man: Tell us about it.

Marta: Well, it works like this: you decide on a menu – obviously you have to be able to cook – then you advertise it so people can book a meal. The most amazing thing is all the advertising's done through social-networking websites. People set up tables in their sitting-room, or in a city car park, an empty factory – anywhere in fact. And because you know how many people you're cooking for, food doesn't get wasted.

Man: So why was it good for you?

Marta: Well, various reasons. Like, I could buy all the ingredients without risk because you make customers pay in advance. The greatest advantage, though, is by having a maximum of ten customers, I didn't need to hire a waiter. Then, of course, I could prepare everything at home – just take a camping gas cooker with me, plus some plates, glasses, knives and forks.

Man: Do you never run into problems?

Marta: The whole experience is fun. People watch you cook and the atmosphere's relaxed. I did one meal on a beach which almost went wrong because I didn't think about the wind blowing sand into people's food. Fortunately, I'd brought a large umbrella to protect myself from the sun, so I put it around their table instead!

Man:	And you sometimes use your own flat?
Marta:	If the weather's bad, people come to my home instead, but it gets very crowded. Even though I've actually got enough chairs and a big table, it's not ideal. I was worried we might disturb the neighbours, but they've been alright about it. I love the temporary feel of the mobile idea, so home's not really what it's about.
Man:	So, what's the future of mobile restaurants?
Marta:	Well, it's rather uncertain. Lots of new ones are popping up because it's become fashionable. I think health inspectors will want to check them out. That doesn't worry me, because I'm a trained chef. But if someone got ill in a less serious one, we might all get a bad name. So I guess inspections are a good thing.

[Pause]

Now listen again.

[The recording is repeated]

[Pause]

That is the end of Part 2.

[Pause]

PART 3   *Now turn to Part 3, questions 14 to 19.*

You will hear an announcement about an outdoor cinema.

For each question, fill in the missing information in the numbered space.

You now have 20 seconds to look at Part 3.

[Pause]

Now we are ready to start. Listen carefully. You will hear the recording twice.

Man:	For those of you who love watching films, let me tell you about a new outdoor summer cinema that opens later this week. It's been set up in the hills with beautiful views in all directions. The size of the cinema screen is fantastic, and the quality of the sound system is so good you forget that you're outdoors. What's so amazing is that you can enjoy the sunset at the same time as you're watching a film!
	There are no seats because members of the audience can sit on the ground wherever they like. The temperatures don't drop in the evenings during summer, so you won't need a blanket, but I do suggest taking a cushion with you because it can get rather uncomfortable after the first hour or two of sitting there.
	So, how do you get to this cinema from the city? If you have a car, then there's plenty of parking spaces and the round trip is about eight kilometres. Otherwise, you'll need to rely on public transport, unless that is, you have enough energy for a five-kilometre walk along a narrow path.
	When I visited earlier this week, I saw that some people had brought a picnic with them. The perfect thing to enjoy after the movie. Some other people tried to light a barbecue – but that's against the rules, I'm afraid – so not such a good idea.
	And one final word of advice. It's not a good idea to arrive at this outdoor cinema without a ticket because numbers are limited for health-and-safety reasons. Tickets are available from any supermarket in the city, or you can get them online from the website, cityents dot org. That's C-I-T-Y-E-N-T-S dot org. So, have fun …

[Pause]

Now listen again.

[The recording is repeated]

[Pause]

That is the end of Part 3.

[Pause]

PART 4   *Now turn to Part 4, questions 20 to 25.*

Look at the six sentences for this part. You will hear a woman called Laura and a man called Karl talking about living away from home whilst studying at university.

Decide if each sentence is correct or incorrect. If it is correct, put a tick in the box under A for YES. If it is not correct, put a tick in the box under B for NO.

You now have 20 seconds to look at the questions for Part 4.

[Pause]

Now we are ready to start. Listen carefully. You will hear the recording twice.

Laura: Hello Karl! I haven't seen you since we both went away to study.

Karl: Hello Laura, good to see you. I'm just back home for a few days.

Laura: Yeah, me too. How are you finding it studying in a foreign country?

Karl: It's taken me a couple of weeks to find somewhere to live. I had to find my own accommodation, although the university was very helpful and gave me a list of apartments so it wasn't that hard.

Laura: Isn't it a problem not being able to speak the language?

Karl: Well, there's lots of students from different countries and we all use English. Anyway, my course is taught in English. But understanding the other students' jokes isn't always easy!

Laura: Sounds like fun, though! Well, I'm really concentrating on my studies at the moment because I've got an important essay to write. I was told how much work there'd be and so I've really managed to get myself organised.

Karl: Yes, time management is essential. Have you thought about what you'll do after your university course finishes?

Laura: It's still a long way off. How about you? Do you think you'll come back home to work after your graduation?

Karl: I haven't made up my mind actually. I've heard that some employers may not accept qualifications from another country. But my parents would prefer it if I came back here.

Laura: I guess you must feel lonely sometimes. I thought I'd love the freedom of being away from home, but it can be hard. If I saw my parents more often, I'd be happier.

Karl: Well, it's normal to feel like that. At times, I felt frightened in case I was making a mistake by going to university abroad. Why don't you come and visit me when you can afford it? I'll book you into a youth hostel – they're not expensive.

Laura: I'm really curious to see what it's like at your university. I've got more than enough studying to do at the moment though, I'm afraid. But thanks for the invitation.

[Pause]

Now listen again.

[The recording is repeated]

[Pause]

That is the end of Part 4.

[Pause]

You now have six minutes to check and copy your answers on to the answer sheet.

Note: Teacher, stop the recording here and time six minutes. Remind students when there is **one** minute remaining.

That is the end of the test.

Test 3

PAPER 1   READING AND WRITING

READING

Part 1

1 C   2 C   3 B   4 A   5 C

Part 2

6 D   7 H   8 E   9 B   10 F

Part 3

11 A   12 B   13 B   14 B   15 A   16 A   17 A   18 B   19 A   20 B

Part 4

21 B   22 A   23 D   24 B   25 C

Part 5

26 C   27 A   28 D   29 A   30 B   31 A   32 C   33 B   34 A   35 D

WRITING

Part 1

1 not / don't you buy   2 to   3 with   4 soon as   5 less

Part 2 & 3

The following sample answers can be used as a guide when marking.

SAMPLE A (Test 3, Question 6: Email to a friend)

> Hello Alex
>
> I was delighted to hear that you will came to my town. I am so excited! For the beginning I propose to meet at the coffe shop in downtown. After this we could go take a walk in the park, go to a movie and in the evening we could go camping.
>
> Don't forget to take your camera because we will do a lot of photos. Write me back soon.
>
> Best wishes
>
> Irima

Examiner Comments

All three parts of the message are clearly communicated.

Mark: 5

SAMPLE B (Test 3, Question 6: Email to a friend)

> Hello my friend! I look forward to you. On may 17th I expect you to come to my house in Fioesti and from there we can go the zoo and maybe we will visit the historical museum. Take your camera with you, because we will moke pictures and then put them into a photo album. I'm waiting for you!

Examiner Comments

All three points are communicated but there is some awkwardness of expression in point 1.

Mark: 4

SAMPLE C (Test 3, Question 6: Email to a friend)

Hi, Alex!

I really miss you! I look forward to you here. I have a lot to tell you. You have got to come on holiday about me. We can meet in front of the museum, we do a lot of things. I don't know whence to start. For a few days you will live with me. You loving books because we will learn, I wait you!

Carmen

Examiner Comments

All three points are attempted but the expression requires interpretation by the reader.

Mark: 3

SAMPLE D (Test 3, Question 7: Letter to a friend)

Dear Harvey

Thank you for your letter requesting advice about how you should spend your money. I hope the following suggestions will be of some help to you.

It strikes to me that you should do whatever you want with the money, because you won it, not your parents. It is obvious that am exciting holiday is the best way to spend it all, after a long period of hard work.

Moreover, I know that your biggest dream is to traevel around the world, and so mow is the time to accomplish it. This holiday is a big opportunity for you, owing to the fact that you don't have too much spare time. If I were you, I wouldn't miss this amazing chance.

I hope this suggestions will prove to be of some assistance, and I think that you'll make the correct decision.

Look after yourself

William

Subscale	Mark	Examiner Comments
Content	5	All content is relevant to the task and appropriately expanded. The target reader is fully informed.
Communicative Achievement	5	The letter holds the reader's attention throughout, using a consistently appropriate register in letter format. The ideas are communicated effectively.
Organisation	5	The text is well organised and coherent, using basic linking (*because*; *and*) and a wide variety of cohesive devices (*It strikes to me that*; *whatever you want*; *Moreover*; *owing to the fact that*; *this amazing chance*). The use of paragraphing is appropriate and there is good internal cohesion across and within lengthy sentences (see the second paragraph).
Language	5	There is a wide range of everyday and less common lexis (*requesting advice*; *obvious*; *a long period of hard work*; *accomplish*; *assistance*). Complex grammatical forms are used to good effect with a good degree of control (*you should do whatever you want with the money, because you won it, not your parents*; *Moreover, I know that your biggest dream is to traevel around the world*; *I think that you'll make the correct decision*). Virtually error free.

SAMPLE E (Test 3, Question 7: Letter to a friend)

Dear Jon

I would like to congratulate you for winning the competition. I'm sure that it wasn't easy. About the prize, if I were you, I would spend it all on an exciting holiday as You said earlier. To go on a holiday is a great oportunity for each person, and why not take advantage? A holiday in Egypt is so cheap and it is very attractive. There you can see plenty of pyramides and a wide range of cities very old from ancient. But you are free to choose your destination as you like.

Hugo Smith

Subscale	Mark	Examiner Comments
Content	5	All the content is relevant to the task. The target reader is fully informed.
Communicative Achievement	3	The conventions of the communicative task (appropriate register and letter format) are used in generally appropriate ways to communicate straightforward ideas. The target reader's attention would mostly be held but the reader is distracted by the sentence which begins *To go on a holiday* …
Organisation	4	The text is connected and coherent and there is some basic linking (*and*; *But*) and a variety of cohesive devices (*spend it all*; *as you said earlier*; *There you can see*). Although there is no paragraphing the reader is able to follow the message.
Language	3	Everyday vocabulary is used generally appropriately and there is some less common lexis (*congratulate*; *advantage*; *destination*). Simple grammatical forms are used with a good degree of control. Errors are noticeable but do not impede communication (*opportunity*; *pyramides*; *a wide range of cities very old from ancient*).

SAMPLE F (Test 3, Question 7: Letter to a friend)

> Dear friend,
>
> Congratulations first of all, and I'm glad you aske me about your problem, that means we're still very close. My opinion is that you should save money, because you'll probably use in the future. I'm agree with your parents.
>
> You never know what will come in the future. For instance, you should keep your money for possible exams. That it's my opinion, now you choose.
>
> I look forward to tell me what did you choose.
>
> Best wishes!

Subscale	Mark	Examiner Comments
Content	5	All the content is relevant to the task. The target reader is fully informed.
Communicative Achievement	3	The conventions of the communicative task (appropriate register and letter format) are used to communicate straightforward ideas. The target reader's attention is mostly held but the reader would have to work hard in places to follow the message particularly in the first two lines (because of incorrect punctuation) and towards the end of the text.
Organisation	2	The text is connected and largely coherent, using limited basic linking (*and*; *because*) and some cohesive devices (*first of all*; *I'm glad you aske me*; *For instance*). There is appropriate paragraphing.
Language	3	Everyday vocabulary is used generally appropriately. Simple grammatical forms are used with a reasonable degree of control but are not always successful (*you'll probably use in the future*; *I'm agree with your parents*; *That it's my opinion*; *tell me what did you choose*). Errors are noticeable but the meaning can still be determined.

SAMPLE G (Test 3, Question 8: Story)

I will never forget the day I went to see my hero, Lady Gaga, in concert. For once in my life I was so thankful to be tall because I could see her through the crowd better than most of the fans who were screaming at the top of their lungs. When she began to sing I burst into tears. My father kept asking me if I was fine and I simply nodded, too excited to say anything.

I can still remember how happy I was and I can say that seeing Lady Gaga performing on stage was the best day of my life. Even since then I keep telling myself that I am so blessed and thankful that my dream came true.

Subscale	Mark	Examiner Comments
Content	5	The content follows naturally from the prompt sentence and is developed with appropriate expansion. The target reader is fully informed.
Communicative Achievement	4	The conventions of the communicative task (appropriate register and story format) are used. The target reader's attention is maintained for most of the text but some effort is required with *screaming at the top of their lungs*.
Organisation	5	The text is well organised and coherent and some basic linking (*because*; *and*) and a variety of cohesive devices (*my hero, Lady Gaga*; *I could see her*; *the fans who were screaming*; *the best day of my life*; *Ever since then*) are used. Paragraphing is used appropriately.
Language	5	A range of everyday vocabulary and some less common lexis is used appropriately (*burst into tears*: *simply nodded*; *blessed*). Simple and some complex grammatical forms are used with a good degree of control (*to see my hero, Lady Gaga, in concert*; *see her through the crowd better than most of the fans*; *My father kept asking me if I was fine*; *performing on stage*; *thankful that my dream came true*).

SAMPLE H (Test 3, Question 8: Story)

I still remember that day...I was unremarkable in my thoughts as usual. I seems detached from the reality. The smile wich was always present on my face now had disappeard. it wasn't me anymore.

I was walking down the street and looked around. Suddenly I bump into a girl. She smiles to me giving understood that it's all right. That was the moment when I met my friend. Since then she has become my best friend and the one that make me to pass that difficult moment and still helps me.

Subscale	Mark	Examiner Comments
Content	5	All the content is relevant and the target reader is, on the whole, fully informed.
Communicative Achievement	3	The conventions of the communicative task (register and story format) are used generally appropriately to communicate straightforward ideas. The target reader has to work hard in places to follow the storyline especially in the first paragraph and in the last sentence.
Organisation	3	The text is connected using the basic linking word *and* and some cohesive devices (*that day*; *Suddenly*; *That was the moment when*; *Since then*). Paragraphing is used appropriately.
Language	2	Everyday vocabulary is used generally appropriately. There are noticeable errors, especially in the formation of past tense verbs (*I seems detached*; *I bump into a girl*; *She smiles to me*; *make me to pass*) and some distracting errors which impede communication and make it difficult for the reader (*I was unremarkable in my thoughts as usual*; *giving understood that it's all right*; *make me to pass that difficult moment*).

SAMPLE I (Test 3, Question 8: Story)

When I was seven years I met my hero. It was a day of sunday when I met my hero. On that day the sun shone strongly over amusement park. This is the place where I met him for the first time. His name is Clifford a big red dog. It was a cartoon character. It always take care of his owner. At the seven years that I had them then, I was amazed by the big dog.

On that sunday I had the opportunity to touch his fur and he started barking at me cheerfully. It licked me on the face and then I began to laugh.

That was a wonderful day that I will never forget.

Subscale	Mark	Examiner Comments
Content	5	All the content is relevant and the story follows on from the prompt sentence. The target reader is fully informed.
Communicative Achievement	2	The conventions of the communicative task (appropriate register and story format) are used and both straightforward and simple ideas are communicated. The target reader has to work hard to follow the storyline in places, especially in the first paragraph.
Organisation	2	The basic linking word *and* is used and some cohesive devices (*On that day; the place where; It was a cartoon character; that sunday; It licked me on the face*). The text lacks coherence especially in the first paragraph where the target reader becomes distracted.
Language	2	Everyday vocabulary is used appropriately and there is some less common lexis (*amusement park; cartoon character; opportunity; barking*). Simple grammatical forms are used with a good degree of control (*On that day the sun shone strongly; then I began to laugh; That was a wonderful day*). There are noticeable errors, some of which impede communication (*It always take care of his owner; At the seven years that I had them*).

PAPER 2   LISTENING

Part 1

1 A   2 C   3 B   4 C   5 A   6 C   7 C

Part 2

8 B   9 C   10 C   11 A   12 B   13 A

Part 3

14 football stadium
15 email
16 sports bag
17 water bottle
18 shirt(s)
19 BEATON

Part 4

20 B   21 B   22 A   23 B   24 B   25 A

Test 3 transcript

This is the Cambridge English: Preliminary, Test 3.

There are four parts to the test. You will hear each part twice. For each part of the test there will be time for you to look through the questions and time for you to check your answers.

Write your answers on the question paper. You will have six minutes at the end of the test to copy your answers onto the answer sheet.

The recording will now be stopped.

Please ask any questions now, because you must not speak during the test.

[Pause]

Now open your question paper and look at Part 1.

[Pause]

There are seven questions in this part. For each question there are three pictures and a short recording. Choose the correct picture and put a tick in the box below it.

Before we start, here is an example.

How did the woman hear about the wedding?

Woman: Have you heard the news? Bettina and Simon are getting married next month.

Man: Really? How do you know? Have you seen them recently?

Woman: Not for ages. Bettina phoned me this afternoon. She wanted me to be the first to know.

Man: That's great. I expect we'll get invitations to the wedding soon.

[Pause]

The first picture is correct so there is a tick in box A.

Look at the three pictures for question 1 now.

[Pause]

Now we are ready to start. Listen carefully. You will hear each recording twice.

One. How are they going to get to the café?

Woman: Where shall we go for coffee in town?

Man: How about the café near the station?

Woman: That's always so crowded. We can try that new one next to the library.

Man: That's quite a long way. It'd be really slow with all the traffic.

Woman: We could take our bikes – though we'd have to go back and get them.

Man: I suppose so. Or another possibility would be a walk through the park.

Woman: That definitely wouldn't be so quick.

Man: But it's so much nicer.

Woman: Well, if you say so …

[Pause]

Now listen again.

[The recording is repeated]

[Pause]

Two. What has the man had a problem with?

Man: Have you seen my new computer?

Woman: It looks good – the latest kind of mouse and a really nice keyboard. It's quite a big screen.

Man: Only thing is one of the keys I use a lot is in a different position from the keyboard I had before, so I have to take my eyes off the screen and look down to press it.

Woman: I'm sure it'll seem easy to use in no time.

Man: I've only had it a few days, so I'm sure there'll be more new things to learn about.

[Pause]

Now listen again.

[The recording is repeated]

[Pause]

Three. When does the man plan to get up?

Man: I'm going to bed now.

Woman: What? At this time?

Man: Yeah, I've got to get up early tomorrow. I'm taking my class on a school trip and the coach leaves school at half past seven.

Woman: What time are you getting up then?

Man: I'll be up at half past six.

Woman: Are you sure that's going to be early enough? You ought to get up at quarter past.

Man: I don't think I'll need more than an hour, so I'll have enough time. Good night.

Woman: Sleep well.

[Pause]

Now listen again.

[The recording is repeated]

[Pause]

Four. What are they going to order?

Man: What are you going to have?

Woman: I'm just going to have a coffee and a banana. I had a sandwich earlier.

Man: So did I, so I'm just going to have a coffee and a piece of that chocolate cake. It looks delicious.

Woman: It's enormous, but look at the price.

Man: It looks worth it though.

Woman: I might have one after all. That sandwich didn't really fill me up.

Man: It'd be more satisfying than a banana, but not as healthy. I'm sure you won't regret it.

Woman: Shall we order then?

[Pause]

Now listen again.

[The recording is repeated]

[Pause]

Five. What is the woman phoning about?

Woman: Hello, this is Sarah Wright. I arranged to collect a guitar I ordered. I was meant to come this afternoon, but there's a problem. I had to get a book from the library and I've just missed the bus – so I won't be able to get out to the shop before you close. I've got an appointment in the town centre to choose some new glasses tomorrow, so I could come in and pick it up then. I hope that's ok.

[Pause]

Now listen again.

[The recording is repeated]

[Pause]

Six. What are they going to watch first?

Man: Is there anything good on television this evening?

Woman: Let's see. There's that science-fiction film called *Lost Planet* at seven.

Man: That's a brilliant film, but I'd rather watch something I haven't seen before.

Woman: There's a documentary about tigers at seven-thirty.

Man: Oh, I heard about that and I wanted to see it.

Key

Woman:	Oh but look, it's on at the same time as the live final of the tennis.
Man:	Well, I'm sure the documentary will be repeated, and it's no fun watching a tennis match if it isn't live.
Woman:	You're right.

[Pause]

Now listen again.

[The recording is repeated]

[Pause]

Seven. What is the woman going to buy?

Man:	How can I help?
Woman:	I'm looking for a smart shirt for work.
Man:	Well, we have a special offer this week. On these plain shirts you can buy one and get one free. They're excellent quality.
Woman:	How much are they?
Man:	Twenty-five pounds and there are several colours.
Woman:	How much are these striped shirts?
Man:	They're twenty-six pounds each.
Woman:	I'm not sure. I could take one of each – plain and striped.
Man:	You won't benefit from the special offer for two then.
Woman:	In that case, I'll go for two of the ones on offer – in blue, please.

[Pause]

Now listen again.

[The recording is repeated]

[Pause]

That is the end of Part 1.

[Pause]

PART 2   *Now turn to Part 2, questions 8 to 13.*

You will hear an interview with a young man called Jack Salter, who has won a photography competition.

For each question, put a tick in the correct box.

You now have 45 seconds to look at the questions for Part 2.

[Pause]

Now we are ready to start. Listen carefully. You will hear the recording twice.

Int:	Jack Salter is a young Canadian who has just won the young photographer of the year competition. Jack, is that right – you started out taking photos of street signs?
Jack:	That's right. I've been serious about photography for about a year, maybe a year and a half, but I've been taking photos ever since I was little. I probably first picked up a camera when I was about seven, and went around taking photos of street signs of all shapes and sizes. My mother tells me it was all down to my being attracted to the bright colours. I guess she's right.
Int:	Can you tell me a little about the winning photograph?
Jack:	It was the first day of dry weather for a while, and I decided to go out and play around with some new kit for my camera. I started off in my own yard. There wasn't much to photograph though until this butterfly happened to land on a large flower, and fortunately I was able to get what turned out to be the prizewinning photo.
Int:	Were you happy with the photograph?
Jack:	I was lucky actually, because on the camera screen the butterfly didn't look terribly

148

amazing. I could see that it was in a great position and the background scene was nice and clear, but you couldn't see the pattern on its wings because of the size of the screen. It was only when I saw the picture on the computer that I realised how good it was.

Int: What do you think of the other photos from the competition?

Jack: I've seen the work on display with mine and the standard is hard to believe. There are photos of animals and plants from all over the world, and you can see the work of photographers from places as far apart as Russia and Australia.

Int: Has anything changed for you since winning the competition?

Jack: That's a hard question. Before winning I'd been concentrating mainly on taking photos of people, although after coming to London for the exhibition and talking to all the other photographers, I intend to get more into doing shots of landscapes in different countries.

Int: Do you have any advice for young people starting out in photography?

Jack: Don't make excuses. My entry was taken with an excellent camera, but that's not everything. My method is just to get out there, and do it, and you don't have to go far to get the shot, you'll find something. You'll start to love it.

[Pause]

Now listen again.

[The recording is repeated]

[Pause]

That is the end of Part 2.

[Pause]

PART 3   *Now turn to Part 3, questions 14 to 19.*

You will hear some information about a student running club.

For each question, fill in the missing information in the numbered space.

You now have 20 seconds to look at Part 3.

[Pause]

Now we are ready to start. Listen carefully. You will hear the recording twice.

If you're a student who wants to keep active over the summer vacation, you'll be interested in this. The Student Running Club meets every week and is open to students from any college in the town. Come to the football stadium every Friday between May the eighteenth and August the thirtieth if you'd like to take part.

Registration for the club couldn't be easier. If you were a member last summer, you'll receive a registration form in an email. If this is your first time, you can register in person on meeting days but make sure you're there by five-thirty pm at the latest.

A five dollar payment will allow you to run in all the Friday races through the summer, and you'll get a sports bag with the club name on it. If you just want to turn up for one race, the cost is only one dollar.

The club's aim is to show that running and exercise can be fun, not to see who can run the fastest, so there aren't any prizes for the person who comes first. After each race, all runners will be given a free water bottle. Healthy snacks are available at special prices.

Runners are grouped according to experience, so there's no need to worry if it's your first time. Those who are new to running start first, and wear orange shirts; those with more experience follow on afterwards in blue, while the fastest runners wear red.

If you need any particular information on the event, or if you would like to volunteer, you can contact Carol Beaton, that's B-E-A-T-O-N, on 8302195. So, get out your running shoes and get down to the club with your friends.

[Pause]

Now listen again.

[The recording is repeated]

[Pause]

That is the end of Part 3.

[Pause]

PART 4   *Now turn to Part 4, questions 20 to 25.*

Look at the six sentences for this part. You will hear a woman called Anne and a man called Peter talking about a college party.

Decide if each sentence is correct or incorrect. If it is correct, put a tick in the box under A for YES. If it is not correct, put a tick in the box under B for NO.

You now have 20 seconds to look at the questions for Part 4.

[Pause]

Now we are ready to start. Listen carefully. You will hear the recording twice.

Anne: Are you going to the college end-of-term party on Saturday night, Peter?

Peter: I want to, Anne. But my sister's coming to visit at the weekend, and she isn't that keen on parties. I hope she won't mind me going without her.

Anne: Oh, I'm sure she won't mind. They're usually great parties, apart from last year's one.

Peter: I thought you had such a good time last year. What was wrong with it?

Anne: Well, it was fun, but it's just that there were too many people there. Some of them I didn't know at all. And this one's going to be in the new college hall, so there'll probably be even more people.

Peter: I don't mind a lot of people, and it's an improvement on the old hall because there's a lot more space. That should really make a difference, so it won't feel as crowded as the old place.

Anne: I hope there'll be a good DJ – that helps to make a brilliant atmosphere, and it means there's a wider variety of music.

Peter: There needs to be plenty of good dance music, but I'm not sure we need a DJ. They just play the stuff they like, or just the latest music, whether it's any good or not. What about the food? Do you think it'll be ok?

Anne: I hear there's going to be a special buffet, with a top-quality restaurant providing stuff, so it'll be completely different from the awful food in the college cafeteria. I hope the party won't end late though, because it means missing the last bus.

Peter: We can always get a taxi if there's a group of us.

Anne: But everyone'll be looking for one at the same time if it ends at midnight.

Peter: Don't worry. I've heard it'll definitely go on well after that because we've got permission for an extra hour. That'll be popular with everybody.

[Pause]

Now listen again.

[The recording is repeated]

[Pause]

That is the end of Part 4.

[Pause]

You now have six minutes to check and copy your answers on to the answer sheet.

Note: Teacher, stop the recording here and time six minutes. Remind students when there is **one** minute remaining.

That is the end of the test.

Test 4

PAPER 1 READING AND WRITING

READING

Part 1

1 C   2 C   3 A   4 B   5 B

Part 2

6 G   7 E   8 F   9 D   10 B

Part 3

11 B   12 A   13 B   14 A   15 A   16 B   17 A   18 A   19 B   20 A

Part 4

21 C   22 C   23 B   24 D   25 D

Part 5

26 C   27 D   28 C   29 A   30 D   31 B   32 C   33 A   34 B   35 C

WRITING

Part 1

1 for   2 was   3 so / that   4 will / should / do   5 did not / didn't

Part 2 & 3

The following sample answers can be used as a guide when marking.

SAMPLE A (Test 4, Question 6: Note to a friend)

Hi Jerry

I'm so sorry I cannot go with you to the football match. My granny is
ill. So my mum asked me to look after her, while she is working.
I think you can give my ticket to your sister.

Speak soon

Dasha

Examiner Comments

All three parts of the message are clearly communicated.

Mark: 5

SAMPLE B (Test 4, Question 6: Note to a friend)

Dear Jerry

I'm sorry but I can't go for a football match with you this weekends
because I'm in the village. But we can visit another match when I will turn
back. You can go with your father or brother.

Best wishes

Kate

Examiner Comments

Points 1 and 2 are clearly communicated. Point 3 is attempted but the point is not clearly made.

Mark: 4

SAMPLE C (Test 4, Question 6: Note to a friend)

Hi Jerry!

I have problems at the weekend, and I will not go to the Football match. Problems is go to the granny's birthday. You can give my ticket to our class mates or to anyone. See you soon.

You Friend Sasha

Examiner Comments

Point 1 is omitted. Points 2 and 3 are communicated.

Mark: 3

SAMPLE D (Test 4, Question 7: Letter to a friend)

Hi Sam,

It's a really good idea to buy a new bicycle! I remember yours is broken.
If I were you, I will go to the shop and try bicycles. If you find one you like, I
can memorize its name and try to find a lower price on the internet.
In my opinion, buying some things from shops can be more expensive.
The only good reasons to buy from shops it's that you can have your
purses immediately and try or see them perfectly. I use to buy things on
the internet when the things I want are in better prices. Or also if I need
somethings I can't buy from shops. I hope I help you!

Take Care!

Sabine

Subscale	Mark	Examiner Comments
Content	5	All elements of the task are covered with appropriate expansion.
Communicative Achievement	5	The conventions of letter writing (appropriate register and format) are used to hold the reader's attention and communicate ideas effectively.
Organisation	5	The text is generally well organised with the use of paragraphing. The text is coherent with both simple linking (and; Or; also) and a range of more complex cohesive devices used effectively (I remember yours is broken; If I were you; If you find one you like; In my opinion; The only good reasons … it's that …)
Language	4	A good range of everyday vocabulary and also some less common words (memorize; expensive; immediately; perfectly). Simple grammatical forms are used with a good degree of control. More complex structures are also used (In my opinion, buying some things from shops can be more expensive) There are a few distracting but generally non-impeding errors (you can have your purses immediately; I use to buy; in better prices).

SAMPLE E (Test 4, Question 7: Letter to a friend)

> I don't know that can I tell you, because I buy things from a shop as on the internet. But I think if you want to buy a new bicycle is better but it from a shop because you can see it better, and who knows, maybe you can prove it. Also if the price is the same, probably you must pay more for charges and service. On the other way you can go in your car to the shop, and as you have a big car, you can take the bicycle and put it into the car or over the car. In this case I think that the best option is this, but it is a suggest. I buy a lot of things on the internet like a mobile phones or some games, but I never buy something like a bicycle! I hope that my suggest help you!

Subscale	Mark	Examiner Comments
Content	5	All the elements of the task are covered with appropriate expansion. The target reader is fully informed.
Communicative Achievement	2	The conventions of the communicative task are used in generally appropriate ways to communicate straightforward ideas. The register is appropriate but letter format has not been used. The target reader has to work hard at times to follow the message.
Organisation	4	Although there is no paragraphing, the text is connected and coherent, using of a variety of basic linking words (*because; But; and; Also*) and a range of more complex cohesive devices (*you can see it better; and who knows, maybe you can prove it; probably; In this case; the best option is this*).
Language	3	Everyday vocabulary is generally used appropriately and there are some less common words (*charges and service; the best option*). Simple grammatical forms are used with reasonable control. Errors are noticeable but in general the meaning can be determined (*on the other way; put it into the car or over the car; it is a suggest*).

SAMPLE F (Test 4, Question 7: Letter to a friend)

Hi Misha!

To my mind you should not but a bicycle from an internet shop.

Firs cause is that you cannot touch and try it. Second when you'll get it can be not that size or colour that you need or want. Third it'll cost more expansive because you must pay for deliver.

I think such things as books or toys you can buy on the internet. But such things as shoes, T-shirts, pants it is better buy in shop. Because there you can try it on and see if it fits you or not.

I rarly buy things on the internet. So, my advice is to buy a new bicycle at the shop and ride on it with pleasure.

Subscale	Mark	Examiner Comments
Content	5	All content is relevant to the task. The target reader is fully informed.
Communicative Achievement	3	Uses the conventions of the communicative task (register and letter format) in generally appropriate ways to communicate straightforward ideas. The target reader's attention is distracted at times (*you should not but a bicycle*; *it'll cost more expansive*).
Organisation	3	The text is connected and coherent, using basic linking words (*and*; *because*; *But*) and some cohesive devices (*when you'll get it*; *not that size or colour that you need*; *such things as*; *try it on and see if it fits you*). Paragraphs are used but not always effectively (see the final two short paragraphs).
Language	3	Everyday vocabulary is generally used appropriately. There is a range of simple and some more complex grammatical forms with a good degree of control but there are noticeable errors throughout which distract the reader (*firs cause*; *you must pay for deliver*; *it is better buy in shop*; *rarly*).

SAMPLE G (Test 4, Question 8: Story)

> I was amazed when I opened the bag. Inside there were differents things: a pink pen, an empty bottle and a box. I asked to my friend whu she gave me that bag. She answered: " I know it's your birthday next week. I can't be to your birthday party. So I give you thoses presents". She also said that the empty bottle was just for fun, the pink pen was because I love pink (She's a pretty good friend!) and the box is a jewellery box. When we open the box, we can hear a beautiful lullaby. I love this present. I also think of her when I open the box.

Subscale	Mark	Examiner Comments
Content	5	The story follows on logically from the prompt sentence. The target reader is full informed.
Communicative Achievement	5	Ideas are communicated effectively following the conventions of storytelling and the register and format are appropriate. There is an effective use of direct speech. The target reader's attention is held throughout.
Organisation	4	The text is well organised and coherent, using a variety of basic linking words (*So*; *because*; *and*) and cohesive devices e.g. the effective use of parentheses (*She's a pretty good friend!*). Although the lack of paragraphing affects the overall organisation, the target reader would be able to follow the story with no problems.
Language	4	Uses a range of everyday vocabulary effectively and some less common words (*a beautiful lullaby*). Some complex grammatical forms with a good degree of control (*Inside there were*; *the empty bottle was just for fun*) There are a few errors (*differents things*; *I asked to my friend*; *I can't be to your birthday party*; *thoses presents*; *When we open the box, we can hear*) but these do not impede understanding.

SAMPLE H (Test 4, Question 8: Story)

> I was amazed when I opened the bag. There was a fabulous present. I was very surprised to see that. There was a beautiful fragrance. A flower fragrance by a celebrate brand. I was very happy because I hasn't got a present. It was pink with a purple flowers on a packaging. I didn't forget this day because there was my first brithday party with my fisrt present. I thanked my friend for this.

Subscale	Mark	Examiner Comments
Content	4	All the content is relevant but there is limited expansion. The target reader can follow the storyline and is informed on the whole.
Communicative Achievement	4	The target reader's attention is mostly held but the reader is distracted by *A flower fragrance by a celebrate brand* and *purple flowers on a packaging*. Uses the conventions of the communicative task in generally appropriate ways to communicate straightforward ideas.
Organisation	3	There are many short sentences producing an overall staccato effect. However, there is limited basic linking (*because*) and a limited number of cohesive devices (*to see that*; *It was pink*; *this day*; *thanked my friend for this*).
Language	4	Uses everyday vocabulary appropriately and there is some less common lexis (*fragrance*; *brand*; *packaging*). Mostly simple grammatical forms with a good degree of control. Some noticeable errors (*I hasn't got a present*; *brithday party*; *fisrt present*) but these are non-impeding.

SAMPLE I (Test 4, Question 8: Story)

> I was amazed when I opened the bag witch my dad brought from the work. I've always wanted a smal kitten or a puppy. But my mum always told me that they would but a kitten or a puppy for me only when we will move to a house.
>
> In two month we have moved but my parents didn't bought me a pet. After several monthes we have moved my dad came home with a big bag and told me to open it I saw a small nice kitten.
>
> I named it Angel becaus it had a white wool and blue eyes.
>
> After school I play with it and at night Angel sleeps with me, I'm happy that my parents have presented me such cute present!

Subscale	Mark	Examiner Comments
Content	5	The story follows on from the prompt sentence and the target reader is fully informed.
Communicative Achievement	3	The ideas are connected using an appropriate format and register. However, the target reader is distracted at times by errors in verb tenses (*only when we will move*; *In two month we have moved*) and the lack of punctuation, for example in the fourth paragraph.
Organisation	3	The story is connected and coherent using basic linking words (*But*; *and*; *becaus*) and limited cohesive devices (*a kitten or a puppy for me*; *told me to open it*; *I play with it and at night Angel sleeps with me*; *such cute present*). Paragraphs are used but not always effectively as they are mostly short and the text appears fragmented.
Language	2	In general everyday vocabulary is used appropriately. There are spelling errors in common words (*smal monthes*; *becaus*) but these do not impede. Simple grammatical forms are used with reasonable control, although there are repeated problems with tenses (*After several monthes we have moved*; *my parents didn't bought me a pet*) and a number of distracting errors (*the bag witch*; *they would but a kitten*; *such cute present*).

Key

PAPER 2   LISTENING

Part 1
1 B   2 C   3 A   4 C   5 A   6 B   7 B

Part 2
8 B   9 C   10 C   11 B   12 A   13 A

Part 3
14 tent
15 meals
16 path
17 map
18 rabbits
19 flight

Part 4
20 A   21 A   22 B   23 A   24 B   25 B

Test 4 Transcript

This is the Cambridge English: Preliminary, Test 4.

There are four parts to the test. You will hear each part twice. For each part of the test there will be time for you to look through the questions and time for you to check your answers.

Write your answers on the question paper. You will have six minutes at the end of the test to copy your answers onto the answer sheet.

The recording will now be stopped.

Please ask any questions now, because you must not speak during the test.

[Pause]

Now open your question paper and look at Part 1.

[Pause]

There are seven questions in this part. For each question there are three pictures and a short recording. Choose the correct picture and put a tick in the box below it.

Before we start, here is an example.

Where did the man leave his camera?

Man: Oh no! I haven't got my camera!

Woman: But you used it just now to take a photograph of the fountain.

Man: Oh I remember, I put it down on the steps while I put my coat on.

Woman: Well, let's drive back quickly – it might still be there.

[Pause]

The first picture is correct so there is a tick in box A.

Look at the three pictures for question 1 now.

[Pause]

Now we are ready to start. Listen carefully. You will hear each recording twice.

One. Where will Peter give Joanna the book?

Man: Joanna, it's Peter. You left your book behind after the lecture at college. If you need it tonight I could bring it round on my way home. I'm a bit short of time though – I'm working later at the café and I'm just going to my next class now.

Woman: Oh thanks, Peter. I will need it. I could come and get it from you at your work. There's no need to come round to my place.

Man: Great, I start at 5.

Woman: I'll see you then.

[Pause]

Now listen again.

[The recording is repeated]

[Pause]

Two. What did the girl buy at the market?

Girl: Hi there. It's Lisa. I just wanted to tell you that I went to the market to get a present for my sister's birthday. They have everything there – jewellery, belts, hand-made bags, beautiful clothes in silk. I saw a fantastic box, a painted one, which would be great to keep jewellery in, and I thought about buying that for her. I got a blouse in the end though. It's a beautiful colour … and I saw some great bags. I'll think I'll go back next week and buy one.

[Pause]

Now listen again.

[The recording is repeated]

[Pause]

Three. What will the weather be like for the race?

Woman: … and now for the weather. What's it going to be like for the big race tomorrow morning, Mike?

Man: Well, it's been clear and sunny all week, but it looks as if it's going to turn really cold tonight, and with ice on the track, conditions for racing could be difficult. It doesn't look like there'll be any rain until the weekend though, and later in the afternoon there'll be a bit of sun coming out from behind the clouds.

[Pause]

Now listen again.

[The recording is repeated]

[Pause]

Four. What does the girl like best about the city?

Boy: Hi Gemma, it's Andy. How are you getting on?

Girl: Hi. I love it here – it's a nice city. There's everything you need just close by. There's a big shopping mall with lots of fashion stores, and a supermarket just down the street. There's also a sports centre right near the office where I'm working, which is perfect for me 'cause I can go straight after work if I want to. There are lots of outdoor cafes too, and places to eat.

Boy: Sounds great. I'll come and visit.

Girl: That would be awesome.

[Pause]

Now listen again.

[The recording is repeated]

[Pause]

Five. What does the boy think was unusual about the film?

Boy: Hi Melanie. I saw that film *Deep Sea* last night. It was amazing. I learnt a lot about the sea too. Have you seen it?

Girl: Yeah, I liked the boat race, it was really exciting – like when the hero almost hit the rocks.

Boy: Yeah, he only just missed them. I thought the way the story was told was a bit different too, you know, the man actually talking direct to the camera before each scene.

Girl: And the underwater diving scenes were great – fantastic fish.

Boy: Yeah, I really enjoyed it.

[Pause]

Now listen again.

[The recording is repeated]

[Pause]

Six. What happened during the football match?

Woman: Did you go to yesterday's match?

Man: Yes, it was interesting. Jim Simmons had a bad fall near the start, and we all thought he was injured and would have to go off. But he was okay, even scored a goal.

Woman: And I heard a small child caused a few problems by throwing his ball onto the field during the match.

Man: The referee soon removed it. Just near where we were standing a fan tried to run out on to the field too. His friends stopped him, luckily.

Woman: Right.

[Pause]

Now listen again.

[The recording is repeated]

[Pause]

Seven. Which part of the gallery did the man visit?

Man: Hi there. It's Paul. I've been to the gallery to get some ideas for my latest project and I got some good ones – you know, for shapes and so on. Now I need to think about using colours, and patterns. I might go back another day and look at paintings. There are some on the first floor of indoor scenes, with vases and bowls in them, like the ones I looked at on display today. Oh, and there's a new sculpture exhibition on, but I didn't get a chance to see it.

[Pause]

Now listen again.

[The recording is repeated]

[Pause]

That is the end of Part 1.

[Pause]

PART 2   *Now turn to Part 2, questions 8 to 13.*

You will hear an interview with a woman called Amy Rowntree, who works as a fashion designer.

For each question, put a tick in the correct box.

You now have 45 seconds to look at the questions for Part 2.

[Pause]

Now we are ready to start. Listen carefully. You will hear the recording twice.

Int: My guest today is Amy Rowntree, who's a fashion designer. Amy, when did you decide you wanted a career in fashion?

Amy: Well, I started experimenting with the clothes I wore myself while I was still at school. It wasn't until I left school and worked as an assistant in a big store though, that I knew I wanted a career in fashion. It was after that I got involved in running fashion shows.

Int: So, what skills does a fashion designer need?

Amy: Well, you need to know how to turn your first idea into clothes that are ready for someone to wear. It's useful to know about materials like wool and cotton. The essential thing though is a knowledge of the techniques used in creating clothes. You also have to be patient, especially at the start of your career!

Int: What do you find most enjoyable about working in fashion?

Amy: It's pleasing to see an idea come to life when you see the clothes in a show. It's also great to go from being completely unknown, to fashion stores knowing exactly who you are when you ring up – that's the best thing about it for me. It's hard work selling my designs, but it's good to earn money doing something you love.

Int: And what about the current fashion scene?

Amy: I feel that the main aim now is to make clothes easy for people to wear. I understand that's important. And actually sports clothes are what make the most money for the fashion industry. But I think you need to design really beautiful clothes too. I'd like to see more of fashion as a kind of art.

Int: Do you find it easy to think of new designs?

Key

Amy: Oh yes. I get ideas all the time, and I draw them so that I don't forget them. And I take photos too. I often get my ideas from things I see when I'm out in streets and parks. I don't get many ideas from clothes in museums, although I know other designers do.

Int: And are you working on any new projects at the moment?

Amy: Well, my big ambition is to put on a fashion show in New York, but no luck yet! I've been asked to design the clothes for a film though, so I'm working on that. It'll be out next summer. And I'm talking with a big store in London about the possibility of doing a special range of suits for men.

Int: Really!

[Pause]

Now listen again.

[The recording is repeated]

[Pause]

That is the end of Part 2.

[Pause]

PART 3   *Now turn to Part 3, questions 14 to 19.*

You will hear a student called Steve talking about working in a forest in New Zealand.

For each question, fill in the missing information in the numbered space.

You now have 20 seconds to look at Part 3.

[Pause]

Now we are ready to start. Listen carefully. You will hear the recording twice.

Steve: I've always wanted to go to New Zealand. So, when I saw an advertisement asking for people to work in a forest near Auckland, I applied.

I was accepted and flew out to New Zealand in January. At the airport, I met other people going to work in the forest and a bus came to collect us and take us there. Eventually, there's going to be a really big tourist centre where we were. I thought I'd be staying in a wooden hut, but in fact I was in a tent, which I shared with four other boys – two American and two Japanese.

It was summer, so I was a bit disappointed that the weather was rather wet and windy. But at least you could have hot showers in the evening. There was also a professional cook, and every evening he made us great meals. That's important when you're working outside all day!

We always worked as a team, so progress was fast. Our main job was creating a path in the forest to make access easier. They'll need it when the tourist centre opens to groups in another year or two.

I also enjoyed getting the information to make a map of the forest area. Something else that was a good experience for me.

I'll always remember how quiet the forest was early in the morning. The birds were singing as you'd expect but I couldn't believe I could actually hear the rabbits. They ran around in the long grass early in the morning.

If you like nature, and you want a taste of life outside a city, try this trip. You have to find the money for your own flight, but everything else, including special boots, are provided.

Anyway …

[Pause]

Now listen again.

[The recording is repeated]

[Pause]

That is the end of Part 3.

[Pause]

PART 4   *Now turn to Part 4, questions 20 to 25.*

Look at the six sentences for this part. You will hear a woman called Martha and a man called James talking about a TV series called Madison, which is about a doctor who works in a hospital.

Decide if each sentence is correct or incorrect. If it is correct, put a tick in the box under A for YES. If it is not correct, put a tick in the box under B for NO.

You now have 20 seconds to look at the questions for Part 4.

[Pause]

Now we are ready to start. Listen carefully. You will hear the recording twice.

Martha: Hi James, how're you doing?

James: Hello Martha, I'm good. Did you watch *Madison* last night?

Martha: I did yeah. Great, wasn't it? The whole series has been fantastic. The final show was hard to follow though – there was so much happening.

James: You did have to concentrate to keep up, for sure.

Martha: I wonder if that's why the series is so popular?

James: Actually, I think the hero Dr Madison is the reason why it's a hit. He's a really unusual person to have as a central character – sort of brilliant doctor one minute, big kid the next. People find him interesting.

Martha: I'm with you on that. I guess the series is about him growing up, accepting he's got to be responsible and follow the rules.

James: I hadn't thought of it that way. You could see it as Dr Madison running away from his problems, not dealing with things.

Martha: Except he can't do that forever, can he? In the next series, he's going to have to sort things out.

James: Well, the series has certainly got us talking, hasn't it?

Martha: Absolutely! I learnt a lot from it too. The personal stories of some of the other characters were fascinating – watching Dr Madison work out how to help them was a bit like watching a detective at work. I'd never thought the two jobs could be at all the same before.

James: I thought as a character he was very amusing, too. I know a lot of people were surprised by that. But I don't see what's so strange about finding a doctor funny. I don't think I'll ever find the time to watch it all again unfortunately, though I'd love to.

Martha: Well, I'm going to buy the boxed set of the series, so I can watch some of the shows whenever I want.

James: I'm sure it'll be worth the money.

[Pause]

Now listen again.

[The recording is repeated]

[Pause]

That is the end of Part 4.

[Pause]

You now have six minutes to check and copy your answers on to the answer sheet.

Note: Teacher, stop the recording here and time six minutes. Remind students when there is **one** minute remaining.

Sample answer sheet : Paper 1

CAMBRIDGE ENGLISH
Language Assessment
Part of the University of Cambridge

SAMPLE

Candidate Name
If not already printed, write name in CAPITALS and complete the Candidate No. grid (in pencil).

Candidate Signature

Examination Title

Centre

Supervisor:
If the candidate is ABSENT or has WITHDRAWN shade here ▭

Centre No.

Candidate No.

Examination Details

0	0	0	0
1	1	1	1
2	2	2	2
3	3	3	3
4	4	4	4
5	5	5	5
6	6	6	6
7	7	7	7
8	8	8	8
9	9	9	9

PET Paper 1 Reading and Writing Candidate Answer Sheet 1

Instructions

Use a PENCIL (B or HB).

Rub out any answer you want to change with an eraser.

For **Reading:**
Mark ONE letter for each question.
For example, if you think **A** is the right answer to the question, mark your answer sheet like this:

Part 1	Part 2	Part 3	Part 4	Part 5
1 A B C	6 A B C D E F G H	11 A B	21 A B C D	26 A B C D
2 A B C	7 A B C D E F G H	12 A B	22 A B C D	27 A B C D
3 A B C	8 A B C D E F G H	13 A B	23 A B C D	28 A B C D
4 A B C	9 A B C D E F G H	14 A B	24 A B C D	29 A B C D
5 A B C	10 A B C D E F G H	15 A B	25 A B C D	30 A B C D
		16 A B		31 A B C D
		17 A B		32 A B C D
		18 A B		33 A B C D
		19 A B		34 A B C D
		20 A B		35 A B C D

Continue on the other side of this sheet ➡

PET RW 1   **denote** Print Limited 0121 520 5100

DP743/389

S A M P L E

For **Writing (Parts 1 and 2):**

Write your answers clearly in the spaces provided.

Part 1: Write your answers below.	Do not write here
1	1 1 0
2	1 2 0
3	1 3 0
4	1 4 0
5	1 5 0

Part 2 (Question 6): Write your answer below.

Put your answer to Writing Part 3 on Answer Sheet 2 →

Do not write below (Examiner use only)					
0	1	2	3	4	5

Sample answer sheet: Paper 1

CAMBRIDGE ENGLISH
Language Assessment
Part of the University of Cambridge

PRELIMINARY ENGLISH TEST   **0090/01**

Reading and Writing   **Day XX MONTH 201X**
ANSWER SHEET 2   **Test XXX**

Candidate Name	

| Centre Number | | | Candidate Number | |

Answer Sheet for
Writing Part 3

S A M P L E

INSTRUCTIONS TO CANDIDATES

Write your name, centre number and candidate number in the spaces above.

Write your answer to Writing Part 3 on the other side of this sheet.

You **must** write within the grey lines.

Use a pencil.

Do **not** write on the barcodes.

You must write within the grey lines.

Answer only one of the two questions for Part 3.
Tick the box to show which question you have answered.
Write your answer below. Do not write on the barcodes.

Part 3	Question 7		Question 8	

This section for use by Examiner only:

C	CA	O	L

S A M P L E

Sample answer sheet: Paper 2

CAMBRIDGE ENGLISH
Language Assessment
Part of the University of Cambridge

S A M P L E

Candidate Name
If not already printed, write name
in CAPITALS and complete the
Candidate No. grid (in pencil).

Candidate Signature

Examination Title

Centre

Supervisor:
If the candidate is ABSENT or has WITHDRAWN shade here ⬜

Centre No.

Candidate No.

**Examination
Details**

0	0	0	0
1	1	1	1
2	2	2	2
3	3	3	3
4	4	4	4
5	5	5	5
6	6	6	6
7	7	7	7
8	8	8	8
9	9	9	9

PET Paper 2 Listening Candidate Answer Sheet

You must transfer all your answers from the Listening Question Paper to this answer sheet.

Instructions

Use a PENCIL (B or HB).

Rub out any answer you want to change with an eraser.

For **Parts 1, 2** and **4:**
Mark ONE letter for each question.
For example, if you think **A** is the right answer to the
question, mark your answer sheet like this:

For **Part 3:**
Write your answers clearly in the spaces next
to the numbers (14 to 19) like this:

Part 1	Part 2	Part 3		Do not write here	Part 4
1 A B C	8 A B C	14		1 14 0	20 A B
2 A B C	9 A B C	15		1 15 0	21 A B
3 A B C	10 A B C	16		1 16 0	22 A B
4 A B C	11 A B C	17		1 17 0	23 A B
5 A B C	12 A B C	18		1 18 0	24 A B
6 A B C	13 A B C	19		1 19 0	25 A B
7 A B C					

PET L   **denote** Print Limited 0121 520 5100   DP744/391

170

Acknowledgements

The authors and publishers acknowledge the following sources of copyright material and are grateful for the permissions granted. While every effort has been made, it has not always been possible to identify the sources of all the material used, or to trace all copyright holders. If any omissions are brought to our notice, we will be happy to include the appropriate acknowledgements on reprinting.

The publisher has used its best endeavours to ensure that the URLs for external websites referred to in this book are correct and active at the time of going to press. However, the publisher has no responsibility for the websites and can make no guarantee that a site will remain live or that the content is or will remain appropriate.

Aberdeen Journals Ltd for the adapted text on p. 19 from 'Up the creek with no paddle – just a lilo' *The Press and Journal*, 17/7/2008. Reproduced with permission;

Guardian News & Media Limited for the adapted text on p. 79 from 'Catlin Arctic team brave thin ice and polar bears to monitor acid oceans' by Adam Vaughn, *The Guardian*, 15/10/2010 and from 'Trial by ice – what it takes to be an Arctic explorer' by John Crace, *The Guardian*, 26/10/2010. Copyright © Guardian News & Media Limited 2010;

Telegraph Media Group Limited for the adapted text on p. 80 from 'Blue Peter star Helen Skelton to walk high wire above Battersea Power Station' by Adam Lusher, *The Telegraph*, 20/10/2011 and for the adapted text on p. 82 from 'Beginner with Midas touch finds gold for engagement ring in the Highlands' by Anita Singh, The Telegraph 6/1/2012. Copyright © Telegraph Media Group Limited 2011, 2012.

Photo acknowledgements:

p. 16 (6): Image Source/Alamy; p. 16 (7): Emily Rivera/iStock/Thinkstock; p. 16 (8): Goodluz/Shutterstock; p. 16 (9): Purestock/Thinkstock; p. 16 (10): JGI/Jamie Grill/ Getty Images; p. 19: Ian Dagnall/Alamy; p. 22: Imagebroker/FLPA; p. 36 (6): CITIZEN STOCK LLC/Alamy; p. 36 (7): Elijah Zarwan/Getty Images; p. 36 (8): Siri Stafford/ Digital Vision/Thinkstock; p. 36 (9): Goodluz/iStock/Thinkstock; p. 36 (10): Stockbyte/ Thinkstock; p. 39: karl anthony/Shutterstock; p. 40: Jupiterimages/Stockbyte/ Thinkstock; p. 42: Anastasija Popova/Shutterstock; p. 56 (6): MBI/Alamy; p. 56 (7): Stockbyte/Thinkstock; p. 56 (8): vgstudio/Shutterstock; p. 56 (9): Deklofenak/ Shutterstock; p. 56 (10): Elzbieta Sekowska/iStock/Thinkstock; p. 60: emberiza/ Shutterstock; p. 76 (6): Brent Bossom/iStock/Thinkstock; p. 76 (7): moodboard/Getty Images; p. 76 (8): arek_malang/Shutterstock; p. 76 (9): Artmim/Shutterstock; p. 76 (10): Tetra Images/Alamy; p. 80: Paul Grover/Rex Features; p. II (1B): Manchan/Getty Images; p. II (2C): Izzet Keribar/Getty Images; p. IV (1C): Photononstop/Superstock; p. IV (4B): Nordic Photos/Superstock; p. VI (3B): Rudi Von Briel/Getty Images; p. VI (4C): Rubberball/Mike Kemp/Getty Images; p. VIII (2B): Susie Adams/Getty Images; p. VIII (3C): Dennis K. Johnson/Getty Images; p. VIII (4D): Blue Jean Images/Corbis.

Picture research by Kevin Brown

Design concept by Peter Ducker MSTD

The CDs which accompany this book were recorded at dsound, London.